Vitasta

PARTITION, INDO-PAK RELATIONS AND KASHMIR

RAM PUNIYANI

Published by
Renu Kaul Verma
Vitasta Publishing Pvt Ltd
4348/4C, Ansari Road, Daryaganj
New Delhi - 110 002
info@vitastapublishing.com

ISBN: 978-93-82711-76-6

First Edition 2017
Secon Reprint 2025

MRP ₹495

Layout & Cover Design by Vits Press
Printed by Manipal Technologies Limited, Manipal

This book is dedicated to my friend Asghar Ali Engineer

Acknowledgement

I am grateful to Irfan Engineer and Ramu Ramnathan for their painstaking efforts in reviewing the first draft of this book

Contents

Preface

The invitation for the swearing-in ceremony of Narendra Modi to the heads of SAARC countries was a step in reviving this organisation and was greatly welcome. Amongst all the heads of state, Nawaz Sharif was most in news. The Mumbai-based Shiv Sena, an ally of Modi and the Bharatiya Janata Party, first opposed the invite, then fell in line and kept quiet about it. India's relations with Pakistan have never been on the smooth ground. The issue of terrorism, and Kashmir in particular, have been the bone of contention all through. In India, terrorism is perceived to be the handiwork of Pakistan to destabilise India. The roots of many an issue lie in the partition of India, which was the culmination of the British policy of 'divide and rule' assisted by communal nationalists.

India's partition has been a major tragedy for the subcontinent. It has also been a vexed issue, more so today than before. While the tragedy had a profound impact on the lives of the victims of violence, it affected the psyche of both nations. The partition was created out of a curious premise: Pakistan was built in the name of Islam, whereas India was a cradle for a 'secular', democratic polity. Pakistan, whose journey began with one of Jinnah's marvellous speeches, which outlined the state's policy of equality towards all the religions, soon pandered to the military-mullah combine, which in turn was dictated (some say it was mismanaged) by the USA through its Ambassador in Pakistan. In the early 1970s, the very same Pakistan splintered into Bangladesh (earlier East Pakistan) and Pakistan.

In India, communal forces sought a Hindu Nation, working stealthily and unrelentingly for the same. These communal forces assassinated the greatest apostle of peace and secularism, the father of the nation, Mahatma Gandhi. That was an overt operation. But covertly, communalism kept infiltrating into the nooks and corners of Indian society. Muslims were marginalised and held responsible for the partition. Muslim settlements were labelled 'Pakistan'. Their role in nation-building was reduced. Muslims in India became a marginalised minority: ghettoised, vilified and considered as the primordial 'other'. In parallel, Muslim communalism also ascended to worsen the divisive atmosphere, sowing more seeds of mistrust. In the 1980s, there was a shift in global realpolitik. India witnessed the rise of communalisation with tacit support from the powers that be. The unresolved debate about 'Whose Partition was it, anyway?' kept resurfacing. It was a Pandora's Box. It became a convenient prop to engineer a riot or create a political icon. Confusion was crucial. The more the blur, more the benefits to accrue! Facts were waylaid, and very few examined the total process of the partition. An intriguing part of the partition plot is, how the communal consciousness in India and across the border blamed each other, but they rarely examined the machinations of the British. There are a few narratives about the British policy of 'divide and rule', but mainly on the margins, even though it remains a vital factor, which led to the partition and the resulting problems which we inherited.

The colonial rule and economy of plunder led to changes but the eradication of feudal classes and feudal values did not take place. The status quo was maintained. The clergy's grip was vice-like. The process of secularisation remained incomplete.

This created the hydra-headed monster of bigotry and led to

rampant communalism. This communalism stokes feudal social values and glorifies birth-based hierarchy of caste and gender. It also deploys a language which incites people to 'hate the other religion'.

At a basic level, the value system of communalists of opposing streams is identical. Muslim communalism and Hindu communalism thrived on the same set of values, both are opposed to secularism, democracy and basic tenets of the national movement. So it is hardly surprising that two figure-heads of the Hindu right-wing fraternity, LK Advani and Jaswant Singh, discovered and certified Mohammad Ali Jinnah as a secular person. The sub-text to this plot was: the contribution of the doyen of Indian secularism, Jawaharlal Nehru, to nation-building was nullified. Intriguingly enough, Nehru and Patel marched hand-in-hand during the pre-partition years. And in Jaswant Singh's *Jinnah (Jinnah: India, Partition,Independence)*, Sardar Patel has been also named as the culprit of partition.

This was curious since the BJP derived its inspiration from Sardar Patel. In Gujarat, Jaswant Singh's book was banned. After a messy media trial, Jaswant Singh was expelled from the BJP. Earlier, Advani's eulogistic remarks about Jinnah had cost him the BJP's presidentship. The Rashtrya Swayamsevak Sangh, which holds the reins of the BJP, did not take kindly to the pro-Jinnah remarks. It clashed with the mantra for RSS shakhas and cadre: Hate Jinnah, Hate Pakistan, Hate Muslims.

In the wake of Jaswant Singh's book controversy, many scholars, academics and columnists revisited the partition process. The spotlight was on the partition again. One man's ideology became another man's 'ism'. This book highlights the lopsidedness of this debate. And as Kashmir is closely linked to the India-Pakistan tussle, the issue of Kashmir is also dealt with. The history of Kashmir, the accession treaty; Article 370, the rise of militancy in Kashmir do come up while going into the background of the issue. The Kashmir issue is generally in the limelight in both India and

Pakistan. More than once, Prashant Bhushan; formerly a leader of the AAP party, has been attacked by mobs for his opinions on Kashmir. Many scholars have contributed significantly to the debate. Two books of Asghar Ali Engineer and Mushirul Hasan have been reviewed here. A trip to Pakistan to attend a seminar was a very personal experience for various reasons. The major being it is in Pakistan that the place of my birth happens to be. The trip has left a deep impression on my mind for various good reasons, and the experience is included as a small nostalgic piece.

—*Ram Puniyani*
Mumbai 2017

Trip to Pakistan

The Invitation

The invitation to attend the seminar on South Asian Minorities in Islamabad, Pakistan, 'Rights of Religious Minorities in South Asia: Learning from Mutual Experiences', organised by the Islamabad Policy Research Institute (IPRI) and Hanns Seidel Foundation (HSF) of Germany (July 2012) was an opportunity to interact with scholars-activists of South Asia to share and understand the problems and plight of religious minorities in South Asia. At the same time, friends in Karachi extended the invitation to give a few lectures on the issues pertaining to secularism and democracy in South Asia.

There was an added possible bonus of an opportunity and that was to visit Jhang, the place where I was born, just before the tragedy of partition of India. Apart from other things, it might have been an opportunity to see the 'enemy country' in person that drew me to this invitation. My family and friends shared my excitement. My uncle, having come to know of my proposed trip to Pakistan, called me to express his joy on my visiting Pakistan and emphasised that I should visit Jhang as well.

As things turned out, I soon realised that VISA procedures for Pakistan require a separate VISA for each city. To avoid the hassle, I dropped the idea of visiting Jhang and restricted my visit to Islamabad and Karachi, for which I had the requisite invitations. The discussion about the proposed trip to Pakistan with friends and relatives had a standard response, Ohh…! you are going to Pakistaaaaaan… be careful! The impression being given was not only that it is Pakistan, which is masterminding all the terror operations in India, not only that it's a country with terrorists strolling the streets and killing people at will but also that it is an 'enemy country' due to its wars against India, its meddling in the issues of India and it harbouring terror dens by the dozen.

Islamabad

Islamabad sounded like an exclusive 'Capital city' with non-government employees a small fraction of the population in the city. The seminar was very intense as the presentation of issues of minorities is not easy, more so in Pakistan. I was forthright in pointing out that in contemporary times, the minorities in South Asia are having a rough time due to the growth of fundamentalism. In India the Muslims and Christians are not only victims of violence—they also feel marginalised and bypassed in the process of development. A feeling of 'second class citizenship' has crept in, the worst example of which comes in the form of ghettoisation in major cities, their higher number among victims of communal violence and their low and falling proportions in jobs and social opportunities.

The representatives of Hindu and Christian community from Pakistan at the seminar were both priests from the respective religions. In a muted manner they said that they do have freedom to celebrate their festivals though they do not feel a part of the mainstream. One of them also pointed out that Pakistan People's Party is no more as liberal as it was at the time of Zulfiqar Ali Bhutto.

Someone pointed out that people from religious minorities cannot hold the highest offices in Pakistan. Overall, this was a gross understatement as there are cases of abduction and conversion of Hindu and Christian girls. The young of the community don't feel that they have full freedom. While the main speakers were restrained in their expressions, participants from the audience took them to task by pointing out the gross violations of minority rights in Pakistan and they brought forth with full force the dismal condition of religious minorities. In discussion, it came up that in Pakistan, forget Hindus and Christians, even many a Muslim sect like Shias and Ahmadiayyas-Qadiani (the term originates from Qadian a small town in northern India, the birthplace of Mirza Ghulam Ahmad, the founder of the Ahmadiyya movement. While it is pejorative to the Ahmadiyya Muslim Community, it is used in official Pakistani documents) do not also feel secure. As far as Bangladesh was concerned, it was pointed out that there is more liberalism in Bangladesh due to the impact of Sufi traditions. It was, however, noted that seeing the turn of events, it would seem, fundamentalist elements are overtaking liberal trends even in Bangladesh.

We could see the Raval Lake from the nearby beautiful hill. The lake separates this capital city from the nearby city of Ravalpindi (Rawalpindi). What came as a pleasant surprise was the feeling of being at home in the city, the language spoken, the people, the warmth and affection and the food; all gave the pleasant feeling of being very much at home. Food in particular was a fascinating part of the trip, the cuisine there did please my Punjabi taste buds no end. While one learnt that the plight of minorities is dismal in most of the South Asian countries on which many papers were presented in the seminar, one also realised that the human rights activists in Pakistan are very vocal and are keeping the torch of democratic values alight with great courage and sincerity. This was also reflected in the books and monograms on display in the seminar.

The banquet hosted by the organisers was a real treat, an occasion to interact with well-known names in the human rights movements from Pakistan, like IA Rahman. I could also lay my hands on Rahman's booklet, 'Pakistan: Neither a State nor a Nation' which gives a very accurate understanding of the state which came into being more due to the machinations of colonial powers than for fulfilment of the aspirations of average Muslims. Incidentally, in 1946-7 majority of Muslims on the subcontinent, and particularly the poorer lot—the artisans and farmers had stood against the idea of Pakistan.

The banquet dinner was a pleasant occasion for another reason also. In the middle of the lovely food and equally engrossing conversation, I had been so lost in the homeliness of the milieu and the accompanying songs from my favorite old Hindi films that I had to tell myself, oh yes, I am not in India but am in Pakistan. The singing troupe playing the music was very good and the choice of songs from old Hindi films was superb.

Bollywood: India's Winning Card

Staying in Karachi was a different ball game altogether. Here, one was in the middle of different ethnic-caste communities staying in different localities. The segregation of communities along geographical-ethnic lines is a bit different than what is the phenomenon of ghettotisation of the Muslims in many a city in India. Karachi with its broad roads and slow traffic reminded me of our own Mumbai nearly five decades ago. Conversation with taxi derivers is so revealing about the shape of things in a city. My driver was a young man from Peshawar. He had to come to Karachi due to the Taliban nuisance. At the time of my visit, Taliban, in a true fundamentalist fashion, were imposing the dress-and-beard code on people and were killing people for any slight disobedience. This young man told me that they used to organise music and dance sessions and week-long celebrations at weddings. Taliban had put a ban on that. In 2010-11-12, Taliban intimidation forced large segments of the population to shift from Peshawar to Karachi. The young man also told me about what many Indian writers were calling 'soft power of India', Bollywood. For this young man, like most of the people there, the three Khans of our Bollywood were semi gods. The young man told me that he celebrated when Shah Rukh Khan's team won in IPL and sported a Mangal Pandey moustache and kept his hair like Mangal Pandey, as depicted in the film. It's no secret that Hindi films and Indian music are a big craze in Pakistan.

There were many talks lined up for me. One was in a college, another for a human rights group, one at the Karachi Medical Association, one in Karachi University and one in the Karachi Press Club. I thought of speaking in English. The first one I delivered in English and was a bit surprised that the response was not very good. Then, I thought of trying in Hindustani, or our Hindi as spoken in films. I found the audience more comfortable with this language. There is an associated anecdote related to language (Hindi-English) in the talks. A couple of years later, I was speaking in a social platform in Hyderabad (India). I was asked to speak in English. The content of my talk was more or less similar (secularism-democracy) as in Karachi. When I stated my opinion about the Muslim League and Jinnah, somebody from the audience challenged me, asking if I could speak in a similar manner in Pakistan. I replied, yes I have spoken similar things in Pakistan; the only difference being that in India, I am speaking in English while in Pakistan I was talking in Hindi-Hindustani!

The content of my lectures was woven around the issues related to Partition, rise of communal politics in India, the role of communal organisations, the nature of politics of the Hindu Mahasabha-RSS-Muslim League (Jinnah) and so on. Most of the post-lecture discussions were very amicable and a broad acceptance of secular-democratic values was evident. I did formulate that the nature of politics of the Muslim League and Hindu Mahsabha-RSS had many similarities. I was told that the word 'secularism' is taken more as a gaali (expletive) in Pakistan as it has been translated as laadiniyat (atheism) in Urdu. I took pains to explain that secularism and atheism are separate concepts. Devout religious people can also be secular like Maulana Abul Kalam Azad and Mohandas Karamchand Gandhi. The non-practicing and atheist Hindus or Muslims like Jinnah and Savarkar can also be communal. I was also reminded as to how communal forces are, in a similar way, denigrating the word 'secularism' in India by calling it pseudo-secular and later further trying to demean it by coining the term 'sickular'.

While talking on Jinnah, the mention of his speech of 11th August 1947 in the Constituent Assembly came up. I was asked as to how I can call Jinnah communal in the light of this speech ('You are free; you are free to go to your temples, you are free to go to your mosques or to any other place or worship in this state of Pakistan. You may belong to any religion or caste or creed that has nothing to do with the business of the state.')? I conceded that this is one of the most brilliant expositions of secularism. This is what later on impressed the BJP leader Lal Krishna Advani also. The problem is at the level of the social base and politics, as practiced by Jinnah-Muslim League and his demand for Pakistan. Muslim League began with the Muslim landlords and Nawabs and never took up the material issues of the average poor Muslims. In that sense, Jinnah can be called a person with a 'secular soul and communal body', and soon after his death, communal elements took over Pakistan and later with Zia UL Haq, the Islamisation of Pakistan was taken to much worse limits.

I found Karachi University campus very spread out, with a beautiful landscape. While talking there, the point came up that the 'process of secularisation' has remained half way through in the whole of South Asia. The British, who colonized the subcontinent, brought in industrialisation and education which are the foundation of modern democratic society. At the same time they let the feudal lords and kings to continue their rule over the masses, which formed the base of communal politics. In many European countries, the overthrowing of the landlord-clergy was complete in the 20th century, but not in the Indian subcontinent. This presentation was followed by a long discussion as the academic community at the university found my ideas unusual.

The very concept of an Islamic state also meets its nemesis in the form of the Mohajir Qaumi Movement. This movement has base in the Muslims who came to Pakistan from India. They could not get due rights in Pakistan and are now organised to demand representation in Pakistan's Senate and corporations. I did get a chance to visit their office and meet the local leaders. The legendary Karachi press club has been able to maintain its independence despite pressure from the military, and it keeps inviting the diverse speakers to talk about their views on matters controversial, on the lines which may be against the ideas of ruling cliques. One of the favourite talk themes there was, 'Shared heritage: Common aspirations', where the commonality of our cultural past was highlighted and a need for broad cooperation between these two so-called 'enemy nations' was articulated in a very positive manner. Most of the talks had good media coverage.

At the social level, it was a delight to stay with local hosts and to interact with many of them over breakfast and dinners. Some of these remarkable interactions I still remember vividly. One of my hosts was working for a human rights organisation in Karachi. His two children are settled in Europe and he was happy that they were away from the mayhem of Pakistan. After the Karachi Medical Association meeting, I met a doctor from an interesting family. His father was a school teacher. He encouraged all his five children to become doctors and later he encouraged their mother, his wife, a school dropout, to pursue her studies and ultimately become a doctor. She and her youngest son were in the same class in medical school. I was also happy to meet one of the editors of *Jang*, the Pakistani newspaper. She was looking after the feature Aman Ki Asha, which was a joint collaboration with India's *Times of India.*

Malyalee Comrade in Karachi

I happened to meet innumerable friends who were struggling it out not only to strengthen democracy but also to build bridges with India. One remarkable comrade from our Kerala, BM Kutty, is a very popular figure in Karachi. Kutty Sahib, as he was generally called there, was part of most of the progressive campaigns and movements, shaping and guiding the younger lot to the values needed for a democratic society and secular state. This Malyalee doyen has lived in Pakistan for the last six decades and his autobiography is aptly titled, Six Decades of Exile: No Regrets. Other friends and comrades from the media, trade unions and Karachi University were not only warm but also expressed how much they longed for a state of affairs—where the military can be packed off to the barracks and civilian society is able to have its say through the democratic government.

Introduction

LK Advani and Jaswant Singh

There are many a social event happening when the debate about India's partition and the role of different leaders in the process of partition keep surfacing. One such event was the publication of Jaswant Singh's book on Jinnah. This book did make publication history of sorts and recorded high sales; it was taken note of in many sections of society. It also resulted in the expulsion of Jaswant Sing from the party which he helped to found, the Bhartiya Janata Party. Many articles were written in the wake of this publication, but there were only a few which touched the core of the partition process and evaluated Jinnah in totality. A partial picture generally provides conclusions which are far from true. We cannot just paint such complex political personages like Nehru and Jinnah in the colour black or white; there are subtle nuances which should determine the evaluation of people of the genre of Jinnah. Similarly, the prevalent views harp a lot on the 'who's done it' about the partition process. The multi-factorial nature of such historic events remains mired in superficialities.
Even scholarly works are not free from such selective approaches. The totality of the events as such should involve the historical context, the class dynamics at play, the interests of colonial powers and the aspirations of the leaders of different parties in

the forefront. Unless an attempt is made to place the complex dynamics in its proper perspective, the best of scholarship remains selective and partial.

The events before and after the partition and the personalities involved have been associated with lots of diverse emotions in different countries. The emotions involved with Jinnah in Pakistan and India are very contrasting. The intensity of emotions about Sardar Patel varies in different parts of India itself. So, when Advani praises Jinnah while touring his mausoleum in Pakistan, he is well received there but is removed from the presidentship of BJP in India. His stature takes a beating for good for large sections of people in India. His own appreciation of Jinnah is not based on Jinnah's whole life and work, the trajectory of his total politics in India but merely on the basis of Jinnah's 11th August 1947 speech in the Pakistan Constituent Assembly. The organisation where Advani was trained-mentored, the Rashtriya Swayamsevak Sangh, looks at only the fact that Jinnah carved out a Muslim nation from 'this Hindu' nation. According to the RSS, the subcontinent has been a Hindu nation from times immemorial, and that's the end of the story for them. In shakha bauddhiks (intellectual sessions) where Advani might have been taught lessons in Hindu nationalism, Pakistan is still presented as a breach in the akhand (undivided) nature of India (Bharat). Advani's calculations must have been more complex. They might have been prompted by the aim to project his moderate face to woo Indian Muslims who constitute a large part of the Indian electorate, but this strategy fell flat on its face.

Jaswant's fascination for Jinnah probably emerges from the weaknesses of the Congress and the compromises made while implementing the secular values in the post-Nehru era. Being part of the BJP, Jaswant Singh might have held the belief that nations are based on religion, so Jinnah's final achievement of making Pakistan in the name of Islam might have been a matter of fascination for him. Anyway, he has quoted extensive scholarship to harp on a few points where the Nehru-Patel leadership precipitated matters in the direction of partition, and that forms the basis of Jaswant's understanding of Jinnah. His extensive work, while very deep in referencing etc. totally overlooks the class nature of communal parties and the goals of the British Policy of 'divide and rule' and their interests in the region. The need for a holistic approach to the issue is very essential to the understanding of the current situation, both in India and Pakistan vis-à-vis each other and Kashmir.

Partition Politics

The Indian subcontinent has been the cradle of multiple cultures and traditions. At times, the kings from this region have extended their boundaries to Kabul and Kandhar; at times the invading kings have set up their empires here. At no point in time has a single king or emperor ruled the entire subcontinent. The migration of the Aryans to this region from the Arctic zone did result in the native-Aryan conflict and later interaction with natives. The Muslim kings, Ghulams, Khiljis, Gaznis and Gaznaavids and the Mughals did try to increase their empires as much as possible, still many local kingdoms survived. The fights of all these kings were not along religious lines. The power alliances cut across the religious boundaries. The interaction of people went on increasing, resulting in syncretic interactive cultures. Since it was the era of kingdoms, politics was not based on popular representation, loyalty to kings was the primary identity of the subjects of the kings who were their sovereigns.

When the British came, they started conquering region after region with their superior fire power. Barring a few small kingdoms, the country came under British rule for whom plunder of the country was the primary goal. In contrast to the Muslims kings, who settled here, the British were always clear in their goal that they had to loot the raw materials and plunder this land. With this as objective, they introduced transport systems and the railways, newer means of communication and modern education, resulting in the coming into being of new social classes, industrialist-businessmen, workers and educated middle classes. The old grouping of landlords and feudal lords with their hangerson and apologists also survived. The rising classes threw up democratic streams and the declining classes came up with communalism as their political agenda. These became the two contrasting poles of political values in the subcontinent.

In due course, Muslim and Hindu communalism emerged from the same parent organisation which had both, the Muslim and Hindu elite. Their political values were the same but they also talked of 'nation' in the name of religion. This contrasting notion of nationalism, secular democratic on the one side and communal on the other were the two poles which were carefully manipulated to play the British policy of 'divide and rule' and led to the situation where even the secular streams were helpless to prevent the partition of the country. The secularisation process, the process of land reforms and freedom from the clutches of the clergy remained incomplete, with the result that the political spectrum remained very confused and diverse. Those struggling for democracy, those wanting gender parity or abolition of caste and all those championing the opposite ran parallel to each other. In this book, these contrasting analysis are put forward with equal amount of confidence.

The British did create a situation where their desire to partition the country was a cakewalk. The leadership of the Congress party and the Muslim League, both celebrated the birth of the two nations from the womb of undivided India. In this division of the country, the seeds of future problems in the form of plight of the population, the tragedy of Kashmir and problems between the two nations lay hidden. British colonialists, by now joined by the rising imperialist power of the US, did want to continue maintaining their hegemony and military bases in the Indian subcontinent. This goal of theirs was well met with the birth of Pakistan, which eventually came under the grip of a military-mullah combine. The country acted as the base of these colonialists, from where these powers controlled the Asian continent, kept an eye on the oil reserves of the region and also countered the Russian-communist block. As such, the eventual trajectory of the partition process, formation of Pakistan, was very complex in which the British called the shots from behind the smokescreen of conflicting views of nationalism.

As religion cannot be the binding glue for modern nations, Pakistan broke apart into Pakistan and Bangladesh, resulting in new instability in South Asia. Meanwhile, many a good effort to create a federation of South Asian Nations came into being. After the decade of the 1990s, these federations too gradually became weak and were not given as much importance as they deserved.

Kashmir

Partition, which was supposed to solve the problem of Muslim representation and safeguard their interests, turned out to be the most counterproductive for the Muslim community as a whole. In due course, the Two Nation theory lay buried in the heap of the dead and the oppressed due to Pakistan's repression in East Pakistan, leading to formation of Bangladesh. The Muslims of the Indian subcontinent got divided into three countries. Only a handful of Muslims who went to Pakistan from India got a decent resettlement, the majority wanting to go to or which went to Pakistan in the hope of greener pastures were declared to be unwelcome, and are living the life of second-class citizens, called Mohajirs.

At the time of partition, Kashmir became a big issue of dispute as the then Maharaja refused to merge either with India or Pakistan and Pakistan's army, dressed as tribals, attacked the State, taking over one third of the State before Kashmir could sign an accession treaty with India and the Indian army could move in to dispel the Pakistani army. The treaty of accession later came under strain with communal elements in India asking for total merger of Kashmir to India; Kashmiri leadership sticking to the clauses of the treaty and the Indian government imprisoning the tallest among Kashmir's leaders, Sheikh Abdullah. The alienation which began here was fuelled by Pakistan, leading to a sequence of events which have made the life of Kashmir's people very difficult. The autonomy, which was promised to the Kashmiri people, started getting eroded gradually, leading to the process of alienation and the geopolitical processes led to a situation where apart from local dissatisfaction leading to militancy, the state let Al Qaeda elements also enter the arena in order to communalise the Kashmir issue. Initially it was Kashmiriyat, which was the rallying point; later the distorted meaning of 'Jihad' started a chapter of unprecedented violence. This was worsened by the presence of large contingents of the Indian army, the exodus of Kashmiri pandits and also many Muslims from the strife-ridden valley.

Pakistan too came under the influence of communal elements and with the death of Jinnah, communal elements, Ulema and the army have dominated the scene, democracy the biggest victim of the process. There has always been the hope, however, that democratic elements may come to stay at the centerstage of Pakistan.

Debates about partition apart, the grounds for dialogue between the two countries is picking up. The people-to-people interactions between India and Pakistan have been paving the way for the two countries coming together. During the 1990s, the SAARC, the platform for regional cooperation between South Asian countries picked up and this shows the real direction for peace in South Asia. The cooperation for education, culture and business will definitely deepen the roots of peace and pave the way for regimes which cooperate with each other to solve the regional problems. This will also start the process of deepening of the dynamics of democracy in the region. The ghost of partition can be laid to rest only through mutual trust and cooperation; the role of any Super Power in playing a divisive role and its agenda to plunder oil resources from the region need to be opposed. The region needs a period of stability and growth for the people of these countries to overcome and heal the scars of the partition process, something which has tormented the area no end.

PARTITION

Jinnah, Nehru and the Ghost of India's Partition

Controversies over India's Partition

The partition of India has been haunting the Indian and South Asian psyche time and time again. Jaswant Singh of the BJP, in his book, *Jinnah: Independence, India, Partition* (Rupa, August 2009) presents Singh's version of the partition process and his evaluation of Mohammad Ali Jinnah, not only as a great man but as a secular person. According to Singh, Jinnah was not responsible for the partition process but Nehru and Patel were the culprits. He also went on to praise Jinnah, stating that, 'I admire certain aspects of his (Jinnah) personality… we needed a demon because in the 20th Century, the most telling event in the subcontinent was the partition of the country'. (TOI Mumbai, 17 August 2009.) This formulation was so very contrary to the popularly held belief in India that the BJP could not stomach it and expelled him from the party. Singh also stated that Jinnah has been demonised in India and that Muslims have been treated as aliens in India.

Few years ago, Lal Krishna Advani, when he visited Pakistan for the inauguration of the Katasraj temple and went to Jinnah's mausoleum, stated that Jinnah was a great man as he had achieved what he had struggled for and that he was secular as shown by his 11 August 1947 speech, dealing with religious freedom of citizens.

This speech by Advani also shocked the BJP and other affiliates of the RSS. The result was that Advani had to step down from the BJP president's post. It is another matter that since at that time BJP was facing elections and Atal Bihari Vajpayee had withdrawn from politics, Advani had to be allowed to continue in the party as an electoral necessity. But, due to this, he permanently lost his stature with the RSS combine (a group of organisations which owe allegiance to the RSS and are run by RSS-trained swayamsevaks or volunteers).

Interestingly, an ex-RSS Sarsanghchalak (supreme leader), K Sudarshan, also jumped into the debate, upholding Jinnah to be secular. Sudarshan stated that since Jinnah had entered the Lucknow pact with Tilak and since he opposed Gandhi on the Khilafat issue, Jinnah was secular and that had Gandhi wanted, he could have avoided the partition. Jaswant Singh's book was banned in Gujarat on the ground that it is against Sardar Patel. As such, earlier another top RSS functionary, HV Seshadri in his book, *The Tragic Story of Partition*, had anti-Sardar Patel views, but it was sold as at that time, Gujarat society was not as much communalised.

All in all, Jaswant's book raised the debate afresh, and many a commentator jumped into the debating ring, 'Jaswant Singh has done a great service by sensitising us to the importance of a better understanding of India's immediate pre-Independence history. His book and the controversy which surrounded it have led me to undertake a closer scrutiny of this critical period', wrote Arvind Panagariya in the *Times of India*, Oct 2009. This does seem to have been the response of most political commentators.

It is true that in India, the view of partition held by the majority is that it was due to Jinnah, the representative of Muslims, that India had to be partitioned. Despite the partition process, despite the formation of 'Islamic Pakistan', only slightly less than half of then India's Muslims chose to make India there home. However, the Muslims who migrated were probably the biggest victims of partition as Jaswant Singh correctly points out. Over a period of time, in Pakistan, majority of Muslims who were not locals, were pushed to the margins of society, bereft of social provisions and facilities, and this added to the insecurity created due to communal violence and the highhanded attitude of the state machinery, and the police in particular, towards them.

In India it was propagated that partition had taken place due to Muslims, Muslims have got 'their' Pakistan, so why are they here? This propaganda laid the ground for their gradual exclusion from the socio-economic-political arena and also made them the target of communal violence.

RSS-trained pracharak Nathuram Godse, in his book, *May it Please Your Honour*—his confessional statement in the court—said that it was Gandhi's 'appeasement policy' towards Muslims that emboldened Muslims and made them demand and get Pakistan. This was one of his stated reasons for murdering Mahatma Gandhi. While broadly Gandhi is looked up at as 'Father of the Nation', a Mahatma, the Dalits in India look at him as someone who upheld the caste system. Right-wing leaders also hate him, though in public they will not say so. They hate him as they consider him a betrayer of the Hindu cause and supporter of Muslims, their propaganda mill holds him responsible for India's partition.

Though, so far, Gandhi is not spared the blame from the Hindu communal stable, it is for the second time (earlier Sheshadri) that ideologues (Jaswant Singh) have pointed a finger at the iconic figure of Sardar Patel, who is generally held in high regard by most Indians, more so and in a special way, by the followers of the RSS, especially in Gujarat. Jaswant Singh blaming Sardar Patel for the partition is something which many could not tolerate. Some other people hold Nehru's ambition for Prime Ministership to be the cause of partition.

In Pakistan, matters are the other way around. There, Jinnah is regarded as Baba-e-Qaum (Father of the Nation), Quaid-i-Azam (the great leader) and held in highest esteem. Even in Pakistan, there are differing interpretations of Jinnah. Liberal Muslims describe him as secular and for supporting their point they quote his 11th August 1947 speech. In this speech he said, 'You are free; you are free to go to your temples, you are free to go to your mosques or to any other place of worship in this state of

Pakistan. You may belong to any religion or caste or creed that has nothing to do with the business of the state' (Muhammad Ali Jinnah, Speech in Constituent Assembly). The Conservative Muslims describe him as a believer of 'Two Nation theory', and a true Muslim who created Pakistan for Islam and Muslims.

The nationalist streams have seen partition as 'vivisection', and 'imperialist betrayal', and a 'historical denouement' of the two nation theory (Surendra Rao, *The Hindu*, 5 Jan 2010).

Some of the Western and other writers try to present partition as the conflict for state power between Hindus and Muslims (Surendra Rao, Ibid).This work recognises that 'partition was a conflict for state power, and that the British remained reluctant partitionists right till the end'. As Rao said, this book argues that, 'Partition was not foisted on reluctant Indian political leaders but in a large measure willed into existence by them'.

Same phenomenon, so many interpretations, so many opinions! The reasons are obvious; we judge the phenomenon according to our own prisms guided by our interests, and according to our ideologies. The commentators have picked up a few events of the partition process and made inferences accordingly. For Advani, Jinah's 11th August speech is enough to certify him as a secular person; for Sudarshan, Jinnah's Lucknow pact is good enough for evaluating him etc. So, the same phenomenon of the partition of India is differently presented in India and Pakistan. The same Jinnah is looked at differently in different countries and by different people.

There is not only a Roshomon (same phenomenon being looked at differently in the famous Japanese film) effect, there is also the case of the six blind men and the elephant. If we look at the limited span of the trajectory, we will see Jinnah as the ambassador of Hindu-Muslim goodwill but will conveniently ignore that the same Jinnah gave the call for Direct Action for getting Pakistan in 1946, leading to the massacre of thousands and triggering one of the major pre-partition violences. In this, we will see just one of Gandhi's viewpoint in supporting the Khilafat movement but will ignore all his efforts to be all-inclusive in the freedom movement, without submitting to the communal demands from either side.

What is needed is to look at the process from the dynamics of colonial powers, the interests of different groups of people and consequently, the type of role Gandhi, Nehru, Jinnah or Patel could play. Any selective and narrow looking at events will deprive us from understanding the real cause of the partition process, something which operated at multiple levels, and in which the primary and secondary factors need to be identified.

All the same, partition did vivisect the people. Later, the theory that religion is the basis of nation state lay buried with the formation of Bangladesh. While Muslim League and Jinnah wanted a homeland for Muslims, the same Muslim community became split in three countries in due course. The colonial powers who presided over the partition went smiling all the way and achieved their strategic interest's safety in the form of their military base in Pakistan. The Muslims of India got divided into three parts, with diverging interests. In Pakistan, where Jinnah is regarded so highly, his messages started being censored, paving the way for the rule of the military-mullah combine over a period of time. His concept of 'secularism' and 'democracy' lay shattered at the hands of those who kept adorning their offices with his portraits.

The Tragedy

The Indian partition can easily be ranked amongst the worst tragedies of the world. There were many ironies hidden in the historic event. As Mushirul Hasan points out, 'No other country in the twentieth century has seen two such contrary movements taking place at the same time. If one was a popular nationalist movement, unique in the annals of world history for ousting colonisers through nonviolent means, the other, in its underbelly, was the counter movement of partition, marked by violence, cruelty, blood shed, displacement and massacres' (Mushirul Hasan, 2005).

The freedom of India was accompanied by one of the biggest catastrophes of the subcontinent, the partition of the country into Pakistan (West & East) and India. The narratives of anticolonial struggle and its success have got mixed with the painful narratives of partition and its aftermath. Partition remains an unspoken horror, whose consequences are relegated to our collective unconscious. Though India had political heterogeneity, it was a culture steeped in composite traditions. This partition was done on the 'strange' basis of 'religion'. Millions lost their lives and were evacuated from their lands. On the night of 15 August 1945, East & West Punjab, North West Frontier Province, North India and Sind as well as East Bengal and West Bengal were engulfed in violence that went on for months. Mammoth migrations of Muslims from India and Hindus from Pakistan took place under the heavy cloud of violence. The unprecedented violence, which took place, shook both the communities to their core.

For six frightening weeks, a mania for murder, loot and rape swept across northern India. Nearly 500,000 people died in the holocaust and 5,500,000 people were forced to migrate from their homes. Muslim-Sikh, Hindu-Muslim populations that were living in harmony was stretched to the limits of their tolerance by the communalised atmosphere. When the 'trains with dead bodies' arrived in Delhi, it further aggravated the situation with the local populace hearing ghastly stories of the massacre on the other side of the border. People whose families were killed, whose everything was looted, came with bitterness and anger and questioned the existence of other communities in their area. 'We have been driven out, what are these fellows doing here (Gopal Dash Khosla)?' The other typical example is that of Shaikhpura, where Muslims and Sikhs lived in a happy state earlier. With the advent of Muslim refugees from India, bringing along with them rumours and stories of massacre of Muslim innocents, within hours the quiet Punjab town was soaked in blood.

The violence accompanying partition identified women and their bodies as markers for community identity and rape and abduction occurred on a mass scale, reports were there about cutting off of their breasts and they were even killed by their own families to save family honour. 'In the history of communal relations, the year 1946-47 marked a period of unequalled mistrust, acerbity and frenzied warfare in almost all parts of India. Tension between Muslims and non-Muslim communities increased till the cords that bound them together snapped and flung them apart, it seemed for ever. Came the horrors of Calcutta, Noakhali, Bihar and after a brief interval, the tragic events enacted in Punjab, North-West Frontier Province and Sind (Gopal Das Khosla).'

Writing about partition violence, Nehru (quoted in Bipan Chadra, *Modern India*, NCERT, 1990, page 271) wrote, 'fear and hatred blinded our minds and all the restraints which civilisation imposes were swept away. Horror piled on horror, and sudden emptiness seized us at the brute savagery of human beings… We sorrowed for the dead and the dying, and for those whose suffering was greater than that of death'. Seeing the consequences of partition, Nehru had a total rethink on the whole process of partition, '…the consequences of partition have been so terrible that one is inclined to think that anything else would have been preferable. That partition has come and brought in its train other vast changes…' (Nehru, Speech in Bhopal, 9th July 1958, Hasan pg 100).

Meher Nigar Masroor pointed out in anguish, '…today, having seen the lacerated bodies of Muslims, Sikhs and Hindus, I feel the city has become a vestibule of hate. History, it seems, is an invitation of revenge. Religion, it seems, is the license to kill, the greater savagery denoting greater dedication' (quoted in Hasan, ibid). The penetrating observation by Urvashi Butalia sums up the plight of the common people, 'The disconnections between rarefied decisions leading to partition and searing consequences in individual lives, remains one of the most powerful tropes that has been carried from partition fiction into work of Historians and social scientists' (Butalia, 1998, p 10).

The creation of Pakistan was accompanied by rivers of blood on both sides of the fence. It was an epic tragedy with loss of friends and families. 'There were memories on both sides of the living in close proximity with friends and neighbours, of a shared cultural and intellectual heritage, and of fighting together for independence and raising the banner of revolt against colonial rule. The birth of Pakistan, a prized trophy for some, destroyed Iqbal's melodious lyric of syncretic nationalism—Naya Shivala (New Temple)—once the ideal of patriots and freedom-fighters.

It severed or fragmented cultural ties and undermined a vibrant, composite intellectual tradition' (Hasan, 2001, page 130).

Celebrated poet Faiz Ahmad Faiz expressed his pain and anguish in the immortal poem, Yeh Who Subah to Nahin (This is not that Dawn):

This is not that long looked-for break of day
Not the clear dawn in quest of which those comrades
Set to, believing that in heaven's wide void
Somewhere must be the star's last halting place
Somewhere the verge of night's slow-washing tide
Somewhere an anchorage for ships of heartache

Faiz,1971 p.123

What did the Partition Lead to?

The 'communal politics', which was meant to be buried by the partition, assumed more menacing proportions in all the three countries (India, Pakistan, Bangladesh). The breakdown of erstwhile Pakistan into Pakistan and Bangladesh buried the 'Two Nation' theory under the stanching bodies resulting from Pakistani repression in Bangladesh and the Indo-Pak War (1971). The relations with Bangladesh, which was born with strong help and support from India, are not particularly 'friendly'. Gandhi's optimism that this partition is a temporary phenomenon and withdrawal of the British, in due course, will restore the old relations remains a distant dream. Lohia's idea of 'India-Pakistan' federation stands deeply rejected by the communal forces on both sides of the divide. '…Partition cast its shadow over many aspects of state and society after Independence. It raised serious matters of relationship of religion and politics, the efficacy of secularism and a riot-torn society, the place of religious minorities in the new political arrangements' (Hasan, *Legacy* 2001).

With partition Gandhi, Father of the Nation, was a broken man. With the decision of partition he became a lonely figure, '…forsaken by Congress lieutenants and wilfully targeted by the Hindu right for "appeasing" Muslims and helping to destroy Hindus and Hinduism…' (Hasan, 2000, p 7). Gandhi wrote, 'I know that mine is today a voice in wilderness… My writ runs no more… no one listens to me any more… I am crying in wilderness' (quoted in Judith M Brown; *Gandhi: Prisoner of Hope*, OUP Delhi 1990, p369).

Pakistan gradually slipped into the grip of the military-mullah combine, duly overseen by the US through its Ambassadors, with atrocities against minorities and gross subjugation of democratic norms. The military-mullah combine has been in power for a painfully long time and continues to dominate the political scene in Pakistan. Its rulers have used the issue of Kashmir as the distracting point from its real problems. In the name of Islam, it has encouraged and supported mindless terrorism, which has worsened the peace scenario in South Asia. Hindu communal politics has drawn heavily from the existence of the 'enemy' country 'Pakistan', using it as the 'whipping boy' to rouse communal passions by designating it as the source of most of the problems which India faces (militancy in Kashmir, post-communal riot, Bombay's bomb blasts and other acts of terror taking place in India etc). Partition of the country was not the end of communal politics. India and Pakistan fought three wars with massive loss of lives and wealth. The 'illusion that religions can be the basis of state' finally lay buried after the 1971 Indo-Pak War, which in addition to other things, resulted in creation of Bangladesh, ie East Bengal, a Muslim majority state, separating from another Muslim majority state, West Pakistan, to form Bangladesh.

Though the people of India and Pakistan have a lot to share, they remain locked in a state of 'semi-war' situation of hatred, mutually reciprocated. The ruling elite of both countries have done their best to keep their people away from each other and also attribute to the other the reason for most of their internal problems. They have tried to restrict movement across the border, and prevented people of the two counties from coming close to each other. The scope of trade has to a great extent been strangulated despite the great potential for the same. The tragedy of ghastly events, which accompanied the partition, was not the end of it. With regular frequency, communal violence in all its horrific aspects has kept recurring in India with gradually increasing intensity, reaching its acme in the well-planned demolition of the

Babri Mosque by the RSS combine (the RSS, the patriarch, and its infinite progenies like BJP, VHP, Bajrang Dal etc). Across the border, in Pakistan, Jamat-e-Islami, the equivalent of the RSS, has been spewing similar poison in Pakistani society. Both these outfits survive and thrive on the divisions that were 'the cause and the result of the two nation theory'. The onslaught, led by both these organisations, stifles the liberal ethos of society and terrorists the weaker and disadvantaged sections of society.

Perpetuation of communal hatred in a society is an index of the backwardness of a society. It dictates the dominance of vested interests and subjugation of exploited and subalterns beyond limits of tolerance. Such an atmosphere is a severe deterrence to flowering of democratic norms and culture. It is a serious impediment to the growth of the nation.

The Backdrop

Kingdoms, Feudal Society, Medieval India

The earlier kingdoms/empires in the world were predominantly agricultural production units in which the surplus was appropriated by the kings through the feudal lords/nobility. This system was legitimised by the clergy who had a strong visibility in the social space. With changes in the predominant production process (from agricultural to industrial), concomitant change occurred in the political organisation of society and it witnessed the emergence of the phenomenon of nation-states. It is difficult to give a single model of nation state, but broadly, it can be said that it brings about an increase in the size of the middle class, it connects the people of geopolitical areas, it unifies markets in regions, it increases the transparency of administration, it sows the seeds for democratic representation, it begins the process of popularisation and implementation of the concepts of Liberty, Equality and Fraternity in different forms.

Kingdoms and empires had a narrow power base amongst the elite and the goods markets of craftsmen were very fragmented. Power was vested with the king and his word was the law. Kings were, by and large, in collusion with the clergy which legitimsed their rules and the accompanying exploitation of peasants and craftsmen by projecting the king to be the 'Son of God' or by some such divine ordinance. With the rise of industries and the application of technology, the social dynamics started changing a great deal. The rising industries required labour, which was tied to the land. The rising industrialist groups required more political power, they had to displace the nobility from the seats of power, and they had to displace the clergy as the legitimiser of the rule of the nobility and kings. This laid the foundation of vast socio-political changes, which began as 'bourgeois revolutions' in different European countries. The monarchs and kings stuck to the system of hierarchies, '...whose values it symbolised and incorporated, and on whose support it largely depended. Absolute monarchy, however free to do whatever it liked, in practice belonged to the world which the enlightenment had baptized as feodolite or feudalism' (Hobsbawm, 1992, p 37). With changing system of production, 'There was thus a latent, and would be soon overt, conflict between forces of old and new "bourgeois" society, which could not be settled within the framework of existing political regimes...' (Hobsbawm, ibid).

These processes began from the late 18th century, first in Europe, and assumed different forms in various countries. These changes laid the foundation of 'modern nation states', which, accompanied a transition of power to the industrialist-commercial group, they laid the foundation of newer equations of social relationships. They also laid the foundation of 'person' being the central entity of society; citizenship and a formal equality, the hallmark of 'modern nation state'. This is just an abstract presentation of the 'core' of the process of change, and barring France and Britain, even in other European countries this process assumed multifarious forms of transformation.

With the emergence of nation states, or pari-passu with that, nationalism as an ideology started taking its roots, not only amongst the industrialist business combine but also amongst poor peasants, middle and lower class and professional intellectuals. National identity started replacing the age-old 'traditional' local identity because of uprooting of the people from villages to towns, and also due to broader social interactions. 'Every people have its special mission, which will cooperate towards the fulfilment of general mission of humanity. The mission constitutes its nationality. Nationality is sacred' (*Act of Brotherhood of Young Europe,* Hobsbawm p 164).

Hobsbawm points out that the emergence of nationalism reflected much more powerful forces, 'which were emerging into political consciousness in the 1830s as the result of double revolution. The most immediate of this was the discontent of lesser landowners or gentry and the emergence of national middle class in numerous countries; the spokesman for both being largely professional intellectuals' (Hobsbawm, ibid, page 165). This 'uprooting'-induced change of identity was supplemented by broadening of identity due to improved travel and communication, making people aware of the part of the country lying outside their area. This also changed the perceptions of people of their own selves. Their earlier 'loyalty' to the local 'lord', king and the religious leaders started giving way to broader national loyalty and identity. Today, it is difficult to imagine that 'nationalism', which is widespread today the world over, did not exist few centuries ago. People did not have a sense of nationhood, and they felt that they belonged to cities or tribes or groups or rulers. Here, however, one must add, that 'there is no single feature or identifiable factor common to all nation- state formations' (Achin Vanaik, *Communalism Contested*, Sage, New Delhi, 1997).

Transformation Process in India

Before the advent of the British, large part of India was under the sway of the Mughal empire. Mughal rule over India was not total as there were many kingdoms down South and the East, which were not under their control. Their administration was based on small kings, noble lords, zamindars and the like. There were clashes between the kings for empires and even the 'Mughal Empire' faced a lot of revolts from the local kingdoms.

During the medieval period, it was not just the Mughals who came here and ruled. There were many other Muslim dynasties which ruled from Delhi. But at no point of time ever was the whole of India under the rule of a single emperor. The British historians, as a deliberate ploy to sow the seed of divisiveness, periodised Indian history as the Ancient Hindu Period, Medieval Muslim Period and Modern British Period. This was done by James Mill in his book, *History of British India*. As such, the first Muslim king to rule this part of South Asia was Mohammed Bin-Kasim who defeated King Daher to rule in Sind for some time. Later we see a spate of Muslim dynasties ruling from Delhi, Ghaznis, Ghaznavids, the Turks, Khiljis, Tughlaqs and Mughals. It is noteworthy that the Vijaynagar empire was ruled by Hindu kings. Also that Babar, the founder of the Mughal empire, was invited to India by Rana Sanga. The administration of kings was not along religious lines.

'The Medieval period of history is interpreted in two contrasting ways. While Muslim communal historians (MCH) glorify it, the Hindu communal historians (HCH) and the Imperial historians project it as a period of tyranny of Muslims over Hindus. While the MCH project Aurangzeb as the greatest Muslim king upholding the values of Islam, the HCH see him as the most bigoted and cruel king in India's history' (Puniyani, 2003, p 43). Chausalkar (1995, p66) has an important observation to make: 'The communalists used history as the opium of the people. They built up illusions of a great past.' Similarly, Prof Arjun Dev writes, 'The two antagonistic communal trends complemented each other, each finding in Aurangzeb justification of his variety of communalism; the Hindu communalists by believing that Aurangzeb's fanaticism was the final proof of irreconcilability of Hindus and Muslims. The Muslim communalists found him to be the pious Muslim who in a way laid the foundation of Pakistan' (quoted in Chausalkar).

The Mughal kings did not disturb the social structure much. Their courts had large number of courtiers, rajas and zamindars, belonging to both the religions. All the Hindu kings who fought for 'their' kingdoms against the Muslim empire, are projected as 'National Heroes': Shivaji, Rana Pratap, Guru Govind Singh. Many of them and their descendants 'allied' with Mughal rulers, eg. Rana Pratap's son Amar Singh developed friendship with Jehangir. Guru Gobind Singh came to an agreement with the then Mughal ruler. Their aim was preservation of their power in their kingdoms and not to build an Indian Nation, a process which began much later.

The Mughal empire cannot be equated to the Muslim period as, though the emperors were Muslims, the administrative structure was not changed by the Mughals. The old relationship of landlords, kings and vassals was not much disturbed. The prevalent caste system and structures were not disturbed. The top functionaries of state were Muslims as well as Hindus. The Hindu zamindars and kings had good deal of social and political power. In the court of these emperors, which were the highest authority next to the kings, the number of Hindu functionaries and allies was very high. As a matter of fact, the maximum number of such Hindu Rajas was in the court of Aurangzeb who is supposed to be the most bigoted emperor.

All the Muslims on the Indian subcontinent did not belong to the ruling dynasty; most of them came from low caste shudras, were poor and shared their plight with the poor section of the Hindus, So, at the top rung of administration there were Hindus and Muslims and at the bottom of society there were Hindus and Muslims.

Formation of the Muslim community took place in various stages. It did not happen with northern invaders through the Khyber pass. Traders from as far away as Greece, Egypt, Rome, Africa and Arabia have been coming into the subcontinent crossing the seas for at least two thousand years as the Muziris sites tell us. These people were not Muslims then. The trading-travelling tradition continued through time and continues today. A specifically 'Muslim' community started emerging along the Malabar coast when Arab traders crossed the seas and began to come for trade during the 7th Century AD.

The general impression conveyed in India is that Islam came to India with invaders from the north. This was not so. Nor did Christianity come to India with the British but in the first century AD, across the seas, to the same Malabar coast which already had Jewish settlers and traders. The Muslim community was not a monolithic one. There were different economic strata, majority being low-caste poor peasants, and another group belonging to traders, and a very small number of landlords. The difference in the interests of the elite and the poor was very vast. The perception of interest between elite and the poor Muslims was: elite shared different cultural values and had aspiration for higher number of jobs and wanted to make a compromise with ruling powers for their social and economic aspirations. It was similar for the Hindu elite.

It is during this period that, while kings had mixed administration, the people were interacting with each other and this is what gave rise to the mixed culture and syncretic religious traditions in India. The social bonding between Hindus and Muslims continued and India's literature, music, art and architecture flourished with remarkable inclusive spirit. During this period, at the political level, Sikhs came up in Punjab as a separate religious domination and the king who ruled the land belonged to the same faith as its people. The Hindu Marathas came up in Mahrashtra. The political landscape was full of battles amongst kings, and religion was not the motive of these battles but power was. Battles between Guru Govind Singh and the Raja of Bilaspur, battles of Shivaji with local Hindu kings need to be seen in their proper perspective. The Mughal emperors had large number of Hindu advisors and associates, Akbar's Navratnas (nine jewels) had Birbal and Raja Todarmal, and one third of officials in Aurangzeb's court were Hindus. Tipu Sultan had major battles against the Nizam of Hyderabad, the latter siding with the British and Tipu Sultan laying down his life, battling the British. A later Nizam wanted to be a part of Pakistan. Religion had nothing to do with Tipu's patriotism.

People interacted and created the Ganga Jamuna tehzeeb (the mixed culture of the Ganges-Yamuna belt) and other mixed traditions all over the country, Mewat, Navayat etc. The most integrative, inclusivist part of this tradition are, of course, the Bhakti and Sufi saints who transcended the boundaries of religious identities and united people around the moral values of religion.

British in India

Many of those nations, which industrialised earlier, went out to colonise other countries, especially in Asia, Africa and South

America. India was colonised mainly by British, small portions were colonised by the Portuguese and the French. The British 'plunder project' aimed at taking away the raw materials from here and creating markets for their goods. In order to do this, they set up new ventures here in agrarian, commercial and industrial arenas. In these, Indians first acted as subordinates but soon took to modern technologies and with this, a new Indian class of merchants, bankers, landlords, industrialists, plantation owners and brokers came into being.

The British changed the taxation pattern in the subcontinent and also imposed the compulsory cultivation of crops (indigo etc) needed for their industrial growth in England, this lead to massive famines during the British rule. There was a total destitution of sections of the Indian peasantry. Many kings were disgruntled, craftsmen were ruined. Opium trade further intensified the famines. To sum up, the major changes in this part of the world were related to the British plunder project. Export of raw materials, betterment of roads, introduction of railways and communications and finally laying the foundations of modern education were some British contributions to advance their own enterprises. The landed classes and the princes were affected in a different way. Many a princely state was taken over and the rights of the kings were curtailed.

The changes in agricultural policies, extreme exploitation of the peasantry and the dissatisfaction of the kings led to the rebellion of 1857. There were multiple factors leading to this rebellion, which could as well have ended the British rule but for the help they got from some other local satraps. The underlying dissatisfaction was the ruin of craftsmen; repeated famines, the attitude of the British, shift of agriculture to cash crops, worsening plight of soldiers, changing agrarian relations, landlords replaced by crueler usurers and changes in land taxation and many other issues were the processes which created the dissatisfaction. Even the beginning of a reform movement was perceived as an assault on 'our religion'.

In 1857, the anti-colonial anger got manifested in religious language when Indian soldiers of both religions in the British army felt that the British are out to destroy their religion by introducing a cartridges which had to be bitten open and which, they believed, were lubricated with the fat of the pig and the cow, animals not eaten by these religious communities. All this created a lot of anti-foreigner sentiment. The British plunder of local wealth and taking it away was very apparent.

This anti-colonial rebellion was national, not communal in any way. 'Maro firangi ko' (kill the foreigner) was the war cry. Hindus and Muslims, soldiers from both faiths, came together and elected their officers. There were instances when the major section of soldiers was from one religion and the leader of the squad was from another religion. There was no theocratic influence on the soldiers. 'Much of the strength of Revolt of 1857 lay in Hindu-Muslim unity. Amongst soldiers and people as well as amongst the leaders there was complete cooperation as between Hindus and Muslims. All the rebels recognised Bahadur Shah, a Muslim, as their emperor…Hindu and Muslim sepoys respected eachothers' feelings.' (Bipan Chandra, 2009, pg 131.) Bahadur Shah was declared as the emperor of the Indian rebellion and chosen to lead against the British. His associates were Tantia Tope, Nana Saheb Peshwa, Jhansi ki Rani Laxmibai, Begum Hazrat Mahal, Nawab of Jhajjar etc.

The British somehow escaped being thrown out and having recovered, they launched a massive attack on those who participated in the rebellion. Major part of the country had remained aloof from the 1857 rebellion. Kings of Kerala, Kashmir, Hyderabad, Bengal and Punjab etc did not participate in this. Some helped the British in their efforts to suppress the rebellion. Those suspected of having any links with the rebels were ruthlessly killed. As a demonstration, many a man was hung by the neck on roadside trees. The British felt that the major share of rebellion was contributed to by Muslims, and so they targeted them more.

Social-Economic-Political Changes

The British had started draining the wealth of the Indian subcontinent since 1757, which helped usher in industrial revolution in Britain and destroyed the foundation of production in India. They also set up new agrarian, commercial and industrial ventures in which Indians first acted as subordinates but soon, with the Western technology, gave rise to a new class of bankers, merchants, landlords, industrialists, plantation owners and brokers. In 1835, English language was introduced as a medium of instruction; its author Macaulay declared that the main aim of this policy was to create in India, men, who would be Indians only in appearance, but English in taste, opinions and interests. But this process had a deeper dialectic impact.

The exchange of ideas and common urges led Indians towards the newer phenomenon of Nationalism, initially not against the British, but in rapport with the Raj (British rule as it was known as). This also initiated the process of different reform movements, and new associations and unions of economic, social and political nature on the Western pattern. The British education policy had many flaws, neglect of regional languages, of technical education and lack of mass orientation. It was totally tuned to the needs of the British Raj. Ironically, it also laid the foundation of nationalism and formation of a class of intellectual elite who, in due course, were dissatisfied with the clerical jobs and aspired for administrative offices. Many of them saw the doors of civil services closed for them, so they diverted to law, teaching, journalism and politics. In due course, this intelligentsia started demanding widening of franchise, simultaneous examinations, competitive examination for services and Indianisation of services etc. Initially, government jobs were entirely in the hands of Hindus. After the 1857 mutiny, some of the Muslims woke up to this and wanted to alleviate this lopsidedness by appeals to the British. Census conducted by the British employed 'religion' as the major category of distinction, and different sections were labeled as majority and minority, terms unheard of during Mughal rule or for that matter during Victoria's.

Indian Renaissance

This exposure to new learning also laid the foundation of the Indian Renaissance. The positive and negative factors of British rule—New learning, Imperial unity, Western liberalism, (Free) press, modern system of communications, along with racial arrogance, economic exploitation of India, weaknesses of Judiciary, missionary activity and assertion of cultural superiority of the English—filled the Indian mind with a new spirit of 'nation' consciousness. British rule and its policies were always pregnant with contradictory processes. Modern means of communication, introduced by the British, like the postal system, railway and free press played a crucial role in creating political consciousness and promoting nationalism. One of the positive things was that English newspapers in India followed the pattern of British news media, freedom of expression, fearless criticism of official policies and also developed an all-India outlook.

Despite propagation of 'superiority of the white race' by the British, Indians were able to counter it by the scientific enquiry and reason brought in by modern education. Their notion of racial superiority and arrogance triggered a chain reaction, awakening nationalism by making Indians aware of their political slavery. Ill-treatment of prisoners by the British and procurement, by their armed forces, of Indian girls to satisfy their lust, were some of the facts which rudely shook the Indian psyche. It can be said that history is witness to the fact that common subjection to foreign rule has welded together people of different races, regions and religions into one nation. In India's history, the British were the only conquerors who studiously tried to keep their separate identity, and maintained themselves as a governing caste from Great Britain. During the post 1857 mutiny period, the arrogance of the British bureaucracy reached its peak, they treated Indian subjects with contempt, inciting a deep feeling of hatred towards them. The bureaucracy believed in the principle of divide et empera (divide and rule), playing off Hindus against Muslims, princes against people, and educated people against the uneducated.

It is precisely at this juncture that the movement for revival of India's culture emerged, having an overlap with the emerging nationalism. Great amount of interest was invested in Vedic studies, in due course, laying the foundation of various reform movements. There were contradictory trends in the development process. While rising elite had great social mobility, this also shaped the character of the Indian elite. This class passed through two clear stages of evolution, the first was anglophilism, ie consider the alien rule as 'divine dispensation' and a desire for its continuation. The second was that of anglophobism, ie the British rule was considered injurious to progress and prosperity of the nation. The British rule had its plus and minus points, eg introduction of English as a medium of instruction and a free press were British legacies which made India a nation. Also, it gave rise to a class of intelligentsia which was to play a crucial part in the sustenance of nationalism.

With the introduction of a colonial economy, there emerged multiple trends in politics. As per Sumit Sarkar, 'Instances of local conflicts between Hindus and Muslims can certainly be found occasionally in past centuries, just as there are numerous instances of Shia-Sunni clashes and caste quarrels. But communal riots do seem to be rare till the 1880s. That communalism, in large measure, sprang from elite conflicts over jobs and political favour has long been a truism...' (1996, 59, *History of India*). The landlords and middle classes threw up religious national (communal) organisations like the Muslim League and Hindu Maha Sabha, while secular nationalism represented the aspirations of nascent industrialists, section of businessmen and vast sections of the poor peasantry and other deprived sections of society. While feudal structures are based on favour and reward, based on ones' social hierarchy, colonial economy is based on competition for jobs and other favours. It unleashes multiple processes, paving the foundation of industrialisation (secular nationalism), it also consolidates religion-based identities due to the competition for restricted resources and jobs. Many a times, communal colour is given to purely economic struggles. In Kerala, the poor Muslim peasants' struggle against Hindu landlords is seen as an anti-Hindu struggle. In Punjab, the struggle of poor Hindu peasants against rich Muslim landlords was given the anti-Muslim slant. Merchant moneylenders, who were by and large Hindus, dominated the early phase of communal politics. Incidentally, Hindus were the maximum beneficiaries of placement in emerging bureaucracies. This was mainly due to a section of the Hindu community being in a position to take advantage of modern education, and a post-1857 rebellion (which was attributed to Muslim leadership by the British) era when the British anti-Muslim bias was at a peak.

Rising and Declining Classes

The changes introduced by the British led to massive changes in the social and political scenario of the country. These changes, introduction of railways, means of communication and modern education gave rise to the nascent Business-Industrial class, a working class, and the educated classes. We will call them as rising classes, the vehicle of modern values, the values of democracy, secularism, socialism and social equality in India. On the other side were the old feudal classes, Rajas, Nawabs, Zamindars and Jagirdars who were opposed to these social changes. There were some who liked the education and strived for new jobs, but were apprehensive of other changes being brought in due to which low caste Hindus, dalits, and low caste Muslims, Azlaf and Arzals could also be economically strong. There were many shades between these two, the modern outlook of democracy, secularism and old outlook of feudal values. The feudal values were prevalent during kingdoms and were based on birth-based hierarchy of caste and gender. This inequality is structural, fixed, cannot change as it has the sanction of religious clergy who still maintain that the king is the son of God, and so the others are inferior beings. Many political streams emerged from these practices. The first streams, the emerging classes, we will label as Group A and the other ones, the Rajas, Nawabs, landlords, we will label as group B. Group B has been the source of India's communal politics, politics in the name of religion and it was from this group initially that the United India Patriotic Association was formed to oppose the Indian National Congress in 1888. Later, from this UIPA, on one side emerged the Muslim League and on the other came the Hindu Maha Sabha. From the same Hindu communal ideology, RSS also sprang up a bit later (1925).

The Hindu and Muslim declining classes had some difference. Colonial policies generated the growth and economic domination of merchant-money lenders (by and large Hindus). Hindus could take maximum advantage of modern education and accordingly, a place in bureaucracy. Post-1857, anti-Muslim bias of the British gave slight edge to Hindus, who took to modern enterprises/ professions with great keenness. British historians used the categories Hindu, Muslim and Brahmin etc. Indian historians picked up only two of these categories, Hindu and Muslim. Indian leadership used religious consciousness to inculcate 'modern nationalism' amongst the people, eg. with terms like Ram Rajya, Khilafat. This resulted in two processes: (a) arousal of nationalism (b) rise of communalism. We will shortly see that communalism arose due to the politics of Muslim feudal lords, Hindu Zamindars and British policy of divide and rule.

Introduction of Education & Industrialization:

	Group A	**Group B**
	Rising Classes	**Declining Classes**
1	Rise of New classes of Businessmen- Industrialists, Workers, Educated classes	Decline of Landlords, Kings and section of clergy associated with them
2	These Groups form Associations, Bombay Association, Madras Mahajan Sabha etc	This groups looks at new changes with fear and suspicion
3	Their political expression in the form of Indian National Congress	Fearful of the rise of new classes and INC, they form United India Patriotic Association UIPA to Promote loyalty to British
4	In due course other political streams expressing the values of this group come up, Hindustan Socialist Republican Association (Bhagat Singh and Friends), Republican Party of India	UIPA gave rise to Hindu Maha Sabha, Muslim League. Later RSS came up as an ideology inspired by leaders of Hindu Mahasabha

5	This stream was conceptualising for India as a nation in the making	Muslim League held that they are a Muslim Nation since the advent of Mohammad bin Kasim; Hindu Mahasabha/ RSS held that we are a Hindu Nation since times immemorial
6	This group held the values of Liberty, Equality. Equal rights to people of all religions, all caste and both genders	Ideology was based on hierarchy of caste and gender, as sanctified by the organised religion, clergy
7	Participated in Freedom Movement and process of social change	Totally aloof from Freedom Movement and opposed to social change

Changes in Social Values, Relationships

In addition to these old classes, a section of emerging middle classes also supported communal politics in the later period. Some of these were ideologically influenced by the emotive appeal of religion-based politics and its exhortation that one's religion was in danger while others felt insecure for their professional careers, these especially amongst sections of Muslim middle classes. Mushirul Hasan points out, 'The swiftness with which the idea (of Pakistan) succeeded in becoming actualised and the intensity of emotions involved had more to do with political and economic anxieties of various social classes than with profound urge to create an Islamic/Muslim state. Both, in its conception and articulation, the Muslim League's demands summed up the fears and aspirations of the newly-emergent professional groups, especially in Punjab, Sind and UP, and industrial magnates of western and eastern India' (Hasan, 2001, P 56). One recalls that after the partition, it was mainly this section of Muslims who migrated to Pakistan.

The Indian National Congress

It is in this backdrop that one should see the formation of the

Indian National Congress. It was not out of the blue that Sir AO Hume got a 'divine' idea to form the Congress. On the contrary, formation of Congress was a logical culmination of different regional and scattered nationalist groups. 'By 1885, the formation of an all-India political organisation had become an objective necessity, and the necessity was being recognised by nationalists all over the country' (KN Panikkar, in Bipan Chandra's *India's Struggle for Independence,* page 73). The socio-economic changes resulted in 'A new political thrust in the years between 1875 and 1885, and was the creation of younger more radical nationalist intellectuals, most of whom entered politics during this period. They established new Associations…' (Panikkar, ibid, page 72). Initially these groups had a strong religious zeal and caste solidarity, which later gave way to secular ideals. There are various organisations which are worth remembering, like the Bombay Presidency Association, Poona Sarvajanik Sabha, Madras Mahajan Sabha. These organisations being limited in their scope, many individuals started thinking about a national organisation. Hume was afterwards clearly connected with the formation of the Indian National Congress. The truth is that India had attained political maturity, and a national association of a political nature was bound to come sooner than later. Naturally, the move was supported by those who had political consciousness and ideological involvement with the country. In 1883, the Indian Association (under the leadership of Surendranath Banerjee) held a National Conference in Calcutta, which called itself 'the first step towards a national parliament'. This can be regarded as the real precursor of the Congress party.

The founding of the Congress party was not a 'safety valve' for the release of anger against the British rule; on the contrary, it was a natural culmination of the political work of the previous decade or so. The objective of this political enterprise, which emerged over a period, was to lay the foundation of a secular and democratic movement, inspired by Indian nationalism. In the beginning, the Congress passed resolutions which began by thanking the British for their role in industry, railways etc and then went on to ask for the legitimate share of Indians in the working administration.

Remarkably, majority of the regional associations were represented in the Congress and intelligentsia and commercial bourgeoisie formed the main stratification in this organisation. Hume had a definite role to play in the crystallisation of the idea of an all-India political forum which was in the air for a long time.

In the beginning, the Congress party was a small body with few members. Due to its all-inclusive and 'progressive' character, it started expanding fast. It formed its focus on the new classes' (the rising classes) opinions. 'By 1900, it had spread all over India and was regarded by the forward-looking members of the new class as the natural mouthpiece of their aspirations. Its support came mainly from new professionals, with a sprinkling of businessmen from Bombay and of landlords in Bengal' (Spear 1990, p 170). Bipan Chandra, one of the foremost scholars of India's freedom movement, distinguishes between the pre-independence Congress and post-independence Congress. The post-independence one, according to him, is a regular political party with particular class character, class programme and leadership, while the pre-independence one, according to him, '...was the leader of the popular anti-imperialist movement of the Indian people, and its activities in the main constituted the movement' (Chandra, 2010, p11).

In competing nationalism, communal ones were rooted in the elite of the two major religious communities and were later joined by some middle class sections. The movement led by Gandhi had a mass character, which relied on the energy and creativity of the masses, and it took modern politics to the people and had pro-poor orientation. It was not just a political movement for transformation of democratic/semi-democratic type of hegemonic societies but also was accompanied by social transformation of caste and gender relations, which are a pre-requisite for democratic transformation. The INC's movement was all-inclusive, in contrast to the political tendencies coming from elite and middle class professional groups. These latter were based on exclusion of others in the name of religion. So both communal streams stood to criticise the Congress and particularly Gandhi. Hindu communalists targeted it for being pro-Muslim and appeasing Muslims, the Muslim communalists accused it of being a Hindu party out to eliminate the political rights of Muslims.

Genesis of Communal Politics

Along with the birth of the Congress began two opposite, but similar in some way, trends which were against it. The first of these was led by Sir Syed Ahmed who opened his campaign against the Congress in 1887; the second was the Hindu revivalist trends, whose entry into the Congress acted as a damper to Muslim support for the Congress party. Despite the Congress being open to people of all religions, the entry of potentially divisive streams into the Congress, especially of Hindu revivalists, kept the muslims away from it. The ideology and thinking of the Aligarh school were harbingers of a bitter political acrimony, highlighting the religious separation in India's political life which ended in the partition of India.

Prelude to Communal Politics

With the advent of Islam in India, there were many who converted to it for different reasons. Many of these new converts carried into their new religion their old customs and manners, without any difficulties. In a sense, the rise of the communal problem begins with the British colonisation of India; as the British wrested power mainly from the Mughals, they regarded Muslims as their 'enemy number one' and employed all means at their command to destroy this community politically and economically. The Muslim elite not only lost 'their' empire, court language, predominance in army service, jagirs (fiefs) but also their 'hold' over Hindus. Hindus, on the contrary, shifted their loyalties with vigour to the new rule and gladly took to English education. Muslims initially held aloof from new education until Sir Syed began his campaign for English education amongst the Muslims.

Sir Syed Ahmad also started the Indian Wahabi Movement which had a good deal of impact on the Muslim community. This movement, aimed at stressing cultivation of moral virtues based on Islam, opposed the development of a composite culture and aimed at regenerating the sagging Indian Muslim community. It ended up strengthening the separatist tendencies amongst the Muslims, more so when confronted with the Hindu revivalist movements.

During 1880s and the '90s, the resurgent Arya Samaj movement attacked the Muslims with increasing intensity. Leader of the Arya Samaj, Pandit Lekh Ram, went on to condemn all forms of Islam and demanded that Muslims should be expelled from India or converted to Aryanism. Another thorn in the relationship came in the form of the Hindi-Urdu language controversy.

Sir Syed Ahmad Khan can easily be called the father of Muslim Renaissance and reformation in India. The East India Company's government had followed the systematic policy of paralysing Muslims economically and politically, especially in Bengal. They also held Muslims responsible for the 1857 rebellion, despite it being a joint endeavor of Hindus and Muslims. As per Francis Robinson, the first decade of the post-mutiny period was perhaps the darkest in the history of Indian Muslims. One has to see the life of Sir Syed Ahmad in this background. Hindus taking ad¬vantage of English education were coming up in the colonial government's bureaucracy. He called upon Muslims to learn English not only because it was to their worldly interests, but also because it was the best way of defending their religion against the Western attack. His efforts led to a change of attitude of the rulers towards Muslims, change in the Muslims' attitude (from hostility to loyalty) towards the British. He reasoned successfully that the expectations of Muslims, to establish a Muslim rule in India, were illogical and unfair. According to him, Islam does not permit Jihad in a country which permits religious freedom.

Sir Syed Ahmed responded to the obvious advantages the Hindus were accruing and advised the Muslims to be loyal to the British, to take advantage of modern education and asked them to keep aloof from Congress politics. His main argument laid the foundation of Muslim communalism. It was he who first pointed out that Hindus, being in the majority, would dominate Muslims and totally override the interests of the smaller community. According to him, British rulers were needed to safeguard the interests of the minority. This trajectory of thought led to the formation of the Muslim League in 1906, mainly by the Nawabs of princely states, big landlords, ex-bureaucrats and other upper class Muslims. Especially after the formation of the Indian National Congress, Sir Syed had a change of mindset.

Sir Syed, who earlier used to call Hindus and Muslims as two eyes of a beautiful bride, started opposing almost every policy demand to the British government made by the Congress. Many of his nationalist followers were shocked due to this change of heart. His colleague of more than fifteen years, Allamah Shiblli Numani wrote, 'This lion-hearted man expressing the ideas of freedom and nationalism, is turning and attempting to pull Muslims back from playing their part in the national movement' (quoted in Gadkari, p 48).

Patwardhan and Mehta, in the *Communal triangle of India* (p 21 to 24), point out that Sir Syed's admirers believed that he was misled into believing that while Anglo-Muslim alliance would ameliorate the conditions of the Muslim community, the nationalist alignment would lead them to sweat.

The colonial government encouraged Sir Syed no end and also gave generous support to his Aligarh Muslim University (earlier known as the Anglo-Mohammadan College), thought to be a way to pave the way for a stronger foundation of Muslim communalism. 'It was through Government policy that Syed Ahmad was raised up as an advocate of the Muslim community and the Government gave the Aligarh college conspicuous financial and political support because it played an important part in the Government's scheme of political control' (Robinson, p 131).

At this point of time, the British were very uncomfortable vis-a-vis the demands of the Congress party (representative form of government, representation in bureaucracy etc) and Syed's opposition to Congress came in handy for them, in their strategy of 'divide and rule'. Changing their stance, they started encouraging Sir Syed in the formation of an exclusive Muslim educational institute, which later on got crystallised as the Aligarh movement. There are different evaluations of this movement which gave rise to a galaxy of luminaries, which surprisingly includes people like Zakir Hussain, Khan Abdul Gaffar Khan, Rafi Ahmad Kidwai and Sheikh Muhammed Abdulla, who more or less were for composite nationalism despite the dominant current in the Aligarh movement, which looked at the Congress as a Hindu body, suicidal for the interests of the Muslim community. This is not to say that Sir Syed was de facto the founder of the consolidation of Muslim political identity in India. Also, Sir Syed and his Aligarh movement, like the Muslim communalism of which they were the precursor, were only for the upper class Muslims. The immediate outcome of these efforts was the steady increase in number of educated Muslims in government services.

Muslim Communalism

One can say that Syed's liberalism began to erode after the birth of the Congress in 1885. Same can also be said of the Hindu revivalist movements, which in the late 1880s began to assume a more communal slant after the birth of the Congress. This reconfirms that secular nationalism was the mainstream, aspiring for an independent country, simultaneously triggering the offshoots of Hindu and Muslim communalism. It is interesting to read Sir Syed's responses to Congress resolutions which demanded reform and expansion of supreme and provincial legislative councils on the elective principle, appointment of ad-hoc commission to review and revise the political system in India and holding of simultaneous examination for civil services in India. Sir Syed was aware of the fact that Muslims, with little education, would not be able to compete in simultaneous examinations if they were introduced in India. He, therefore, contemptuously condemned the Congress demands for representative government and competitive examinations.

In 1906, a delegation of Muslim elite met the then British Viceroy and encouraged by the Viceroy, they formed the Muslim League in December 1906. Prince Aga Khan, who was elected the President of the League, pointed out that, 'As the special position of Mussalmans has been accepted in principle, the League should work towards concretely defining these rights in every field, our representatives in the council would act as loyal citizens of the empire and the protectors of Muslim matters' (Chandra, *Communalism in Modern India*, p 548).

The British deliberately carried on the policy of ready acceptance of Muslim communal demands. 'The demand for privileged representation of Muslims, through the reservation of certain number of seats in the new advisory councils in excess of proportionate Muslim population, and separate electorate were accepted in full... While the Congress demand for representative government, put forward 25 years ago, was to be denied, the Muslim League's demands were accepted in full in three years' (Bipan Chandra, p 268).

Jinnah's gradual shift to the Muslim League and his communal position also led him to see the Congress as a Hindu body. The 1937 election programme of the Muslim League outlined its intent to protect the religious rights of Muslims in all matters of purely religious character. Before the Muslim League went on for the resolution demanding Pakistan, it felt that the Congress was anti-Muslim and pro-Hindu. That the party could not see from the point of view of the average and poor people, its elite character was blatantly clear. On the other hand, Nehru did not recognise either the Muslim League or the Hindu communalists, saying they were not representatives of the respective communities. This further alienated the Muslim League. In the October 1937 session of the Muslim League, Jinnah remarked, 'The present leadership of the Congress, especially during the last ten years, has been responsible for alienating the Mussalmans of India, more and more by pursuing a policy which is exclusively Hindu, and since they have formed governments in six provinces where they are in majority, they have by their words, deeds and programmes shown that the Musslamans cannot expect any justice at their hands. On the very threshold of what little power and responsibility is given, the majority community has clearly shown their hand—that Hindustan is for the Hindus' (Mehta and Patwardhan, p 43, quoted in Gadkari, p 90). The next jump for Jinnah and the Muslim League was to demand a separate country—Pakistan, in the Lahore Muslim League session of 1940.

Hindu Communalism

The Hindu revivalist movement at this time was harping on 'go back to Vedas', 'cow protection', 'Hindi vs Urdu' and an assertion of 'Hindu Superiority', arousing among Muslims a sense of fear and longing to preserve their culture and identity. It can be said that the above fears, combined with educational and intellectual imbalance from the beginning of the British rule which persisted for a long time, were largely responsible for conflict and tension that took place between the two communities and that Sir Syed was not so much anti-Hindu as pro-Muslim. Thus, Hindu communalism was also born at the same time. From the 1870s, a section of Hindu landlords, moneylenders and middle class professionals began to arouse anti-Muslim sentiments. They talked of the 'tyrannical rule' of Muslim kings in medieval times and the 'liberating role of British rulers'. They gave a communal colour to the language issue (Hindi vs Urdu). They began an anti-cow slaughter campaign, aimed primarily against the Muslims. This, in due course, gave rise to the formation of the Punjab Hindu Sabha in 1909, supported by the Hindu rajas. Its leadership condemned the Congress philosophy of trying to unite Indians into a single nation and for sacrificing Hindu interests to appease the Muslims. Quite like the Muslim communalists, they asked for government patronage and support to fight the enemy, the Muslims. This Hindu communal politics was further crystallised with the formation of the Hindu Mahasabha, whose first convention was held in 1915.

Both kinds of communalism were the refuge for landlords and money lenders. The leaders of communal groups wooed them by instigating them against each other. Hindu communalists were against Muslims being permitted to join the Congress, and they called the Congress policy 'appeasement' of Muslims. Till the 1930s, competitive communalism kept playing its narrow role and got its patronage form the British, though the exact trajectory of this communalism was a bit different. Then Hindu communalists started frightening the Hindus about the threat of Muslims; one UN Mukherjee wrote, 'They (Muslims) are growing in number, in strength, in health...they are waiting for our extinction' (Hindus a Dying Race, Quoted in Bipan Chandra, *Communalism in Modern India*, Vikas, Delhi 1984, p 136). Lal Chand said that Congress politics was following the policy of self-abnegation and self- immolation (Bipan Chandra, ibid). MS Golwalkar in 1939 declared that, 'if minority demands were accepted, Hindu national life runs the risk of being shattered'. 'Those who declared "no swaraj without Hindu Muslim unity" have perpetrated the greatest treason on our society' (MS Golwalkar, p 152, quoted in Bipan Chandra 1988).

More so after 1937, communalism became the main point around which the British could implement 'divide and rule' as by then, the national movement had succeeded in uniting people, transcending the narrow identities of language and region. 'The communal card alone was available for playing against the national movement and the rulers decided to play it to the limit, to stake it all. They threw all the weight of the colonial state behind Muslim communalism, even though it was headed by a man, MA Jinnah, whom they disliked and feared for his sturdy independence and outspoken anti-colonialism' (Bipan Chandra, p 430,1988).

The Communalists: Birds of the Same Feather

While the Muslim League and the Hindu Mahsabha spewed venom against Hindus and Muslims respectively, their core principles were the same. They both were very critical of the policies of Gandhi and the Congress party. Hindu communalists accused Congress of appeasing Muslims and Muslim communalists accused Congress of being anti-Muslim and of being a party only of Hindus. The fact was, Congress had apt representation from all the religious communities. These communalists were also following the politics which never opposed British policies and their major focus was to oppose the national movement.

In his 1938 presidential address of the Hindu Mahasabha, Savarkar accused the Congress of being anti-Hindu and said that Congressmen betray Hindu interests at every turn and keep dancing attention on the Muslim League... (*Hindu Rashtra Darshan*, p 71). So he asked Hindus to boycott the Congress. Golwalkar of the RSS referred to the Congress as traitors, '... Strange...very strange that traitors should be enthroned as national heroes and patriots heaped with ignominy' (Golwalkar, *We*...p6). The whole effort of the Congress against British power was seen as being anti-national (read Hindu). 'These creatures who took upon themselves the burden of leading people and the men of the stamp of traitors such as Jaychand, Mansingh...with same pettiness, selfishness and working like them for our (read Hindus) ruin and playing false to the nation, merely to maintain themselves in public eye...they are degenerated self-styled leaders frittering away national energy in anti-national work' (*We or Our Nationhood*, pp 70-72).

The communalists had a misplaced notion that they were representatives of the respective communities. Despite the Muslim League's defeat at State elections (1937), Jinnah claimed that he was speaking for hundred million Muslims of India. 'When I say hundred million, I mean 99% of them are with us. Leaving aside some, who are traitors, cranks and lunatics...' (*Jinnah MA Speeches and Writings*, ed. Ahmed Jamiluddin, p 567). Jinnah went on to outline the irreconcilabity of Hinduism and Islam, saying they were not only religions but were different social systems in which there cannot be any amity. This led to the Pakistan resolution at the Lahore convention, '...that geographically contiguous units are demarcated into regions, which should be constituted with such territorial readjustments as may be necessary, that the areas in which the Muslims are numerically in majority as in North-Western and Eastern zones of India should be grouped to constitute "Independent States" in which the constituent units shall be autonomous and sovereign' (text from *Communal Triangle* page 48).

Common Features of Communalists

1. Only the propertied and highly placed, educated constituted these groups in the beginning, later a very small section of average people supported them due to their emotive appeal.

2. They never canvassed or supported the demands for democratic rights of the people. The people were heavily oppressed and exploited due to the policies of the British, and the landed aristocracy. They were loyal to the British.

3. The Hindu and Muslim masses shunned these groups right till the end. Only towards the end, after the communal riots of 1944-46, were a section of middle class and urban poor drawn to their vortex.

4. After the departure of the British, some Rajas/Nawabs tried to form independent sates/federation with the help of mercenary forces from the newly created state, Pakistan.

Divide and Rule: British Policy

After the great rebellion of 1857, the British were cautious and wanted to ensure perpetuation of their rule and for this the policy of divide and rule was their chosen policy. For dividing there can be many grounds, region, caste and religion. They did at times play one region against another region, but it was religion which was the most explosive issue and could cut across all other subdivisions; it was this which was promoted subtly and at times directly. The elite of the communities, the landlords and kings, became their vehicles for playing out this politics.

As the Indian National Congress started criticising the British rulers from its platform, the British felt the need for driving a wedge in this national sentiment, and for this, they used the communal interpretation of history.

They took every opportunity to encourage communal organisations, accept their demands easily and never subjected the communal forces to any repression. The competition for jobs, the political privileges in the changing political scenario were used by them deftly, 'The British rulers took advantage of the aspirations of the elite Muslims for playing their devious game of "divide and rule". As the expression of loyalty to the united platform of the Congress began to abate, a communal platform appeared to express loyalty to British more vehemently, the thinking being that in the space for concessions, the more loyal had greater chance to win.... Simla (Muslim) delegation under Prince Aga Khan, which was the beginning of the so called "Muslim separatism", was comprised only of Nawabs and Zamindars (kings, landlords). In demanding separate electorates and excessive representation in councils, they were, in fact, angling for greater share of power for the Muslim elite'. (Gadkari, p 18). Gadkari also points out that 'In a special meeting of Muslim leaders called at Dacca in 1904, Curzon declared that one purpose of the proposed partition was "to invest in Mohammadens in East Bengal, a unity which British enjoyed since the days of old Mussalman Kings and Viceroys'"(Gadkari, p 52).

The British played their cards well, taking advantage of the Hindu-Muslim divide. They kept shuffling their stance to ensure the sustenance of the cleavage right since Dufferin had suggested separate electorates, a move meant to wean Muslims away from the Congress was brought forward. In the Simla delegation (1906) of Muslim landlords and nawabs, the Viceroy not only pointed out that Muslims require separate representation but also that care and caution will be exercised to see that the interests of Muslim community will not suffer, and needless to say that the 'Muslims' for them were Muslim Nawabs and landlords. This was an attempt by the British Viceroy to establish a separate identity for Muslims, in order to disrupt the rising anti-imperialist struggle. Lady Mary Minto, in Countess of Minto; India', (Minto and Morley 1905-1910 p 7-8) writes about the recognition to the Muslim elites' delegation, '... a very very big thing has happened today. A work of statesmanship took place that will affect India and Indian history for many long years'. How true!

The communal divide manifested as communalism in India. In most parts of the world, it has become a political synonym for separatism. Like nationalism, communalism is a modern ideology, which incorporated some aspects and elements of the past ideologies, institutions and historical background to form a new political discourse or mix. It used many elements inherited from the past. It is not a revival or continuation of medieval ideology. It is the politics of declining sections of society to preserve their interests in changing the political systems. For this purpose, they use the cover of religion for their political interests.

In fact, the 'British were so keen on promoting divisiveness that despite the defeat of the Muslim League in 1937 elections even in the Muslim majority provinces, the British bestowed on Jinnah the status of sole spokesperson of the Muslims of India' (Gadkari, p 38).

No community is a uniform community. Muslims have different occupational and other social subgroups, Ashrafs (belonging to foreign extractions): Syeds, Sheikhs, Mughals and Pathans, while those of Indian origin: converts from high castes, Muslim Rajputs, converts from clean occupational jobs like Julahas, Qassabs and from untouchables, Bhangis and Chamars. During Mughal rule, a composite culture had evolved which linked Hindus and Muslims in bonds of friendship and fellow feeling. With the British colonisation of India, introduction of self-governing institutions, the policy of 'divide and rule' resulted in processes which on the one hand razed to the ground the legacies of Mughal culture and on the other hand, generated bad blood between the two communities.

As we will see, the final act of partition was the outcome of the interaction of British policy, Muslim communal interests and Hindu communal interests. To begin with, though Arya Samaj gave a vision to Hindus through the concept of self-reliance, it also created alienation of Muslims through its Shuddhi, Sangathan and cow protection campaigns. Opposition to Urdu and slogans of Hindi, Hindu, Hindusthan further widened the divide. Unfortunately, the Congress presented a dominant secular ideology and also a minor Hindu communal ideology. While extremist Hindu communalists were in the Hindu Mahasabha and the RSS, some in the Congress also equated nationalism with Hinduism.

While Muslim communal elements played a similar role amongst sections of Muslims, eg one Haji Sheriatullah started the Faraize movement, aimed to 'cleanse the worship of god' from amongst the poor neo-converts to Islam in Bengal. The extra-territorial allegiance, though it was more emotional than real, fostered communal loyalties. In the beginning, pan-Islamism arose in protest against European imperialism and was in no way communal in the Indian context.

Partition of Bengal and separate electorate are the best examples of British 'divide and rule'. Interestingly, national historians in India hold the British responsible for separatist tendencies while Pakistani historians regard Muslims as a 'nation' by themselves in South Asia. Primarily, the British were baking their own bread while throwing the crumbs to Hindu and Muslim communal forces. The other major steps of British policy were Communal Historiography and the Macdonald's Communal Award of 1932.

Communal Historiography

If we look at the British polices, right from the beginning, in it there were germs of divide and rule. They saw Indian society as divided along religious lines, underplaying the fact that the real divisions were not along religious lines but along class and caste lines. Shaken by the massive revolt of 1857, their subtle policies of 'divide and rule' started becoming more overt and articulate. In 1858, Lord Elphinstone, Governor of Bombay Province, in his communication to East India Company's executives wrote, 'Divide et Impera' (Divide and Rule) was old Roman motto and it should be ours'. In return, Charles Wood, Secretary of State for India wrote that, 'The [mutual] antagonism of Indian races was an element of strength to British India. Therefore "a dissociating spirit" should be kept up, for if India was to unite against us, how long could we maintain ourselves?' (quoted in Jayant Gadkari, p 54).

Both these quotes amply indicate the shape of policies to come in time. As a foundation of these polices, 'doctoring of mass-consciousness' along religious lines began through specially sponsored history books. The two major ones in this direction were the eight-volume *History of India* as told by its own Historians—as told by British historians Elliot and Dawson—and *History of India* by James Mill, who periodised Indian history into the Hindu Period, Muslim Period and British Period. This periodisation gave the impression that history's period is determined by the religion of the king. 'This periodisation of history did lot of damage in our understanding of those periods. With such religious concepts of periodisation of history, it became easier for them to inject communal poison in the mind of Indians. By describing their own period as the "British Period", they cleverly avoided prejudice against Christianity... Neither there was Hindu rule, nor Muslim rule. It can more aptly be described as dynastic rule' (Engineer, 1998, p 5).

Needless to say that the medieval administration of kings was never based along religious lines; their court officials and chain of landlords belonged to both the religions. The Muslim rulers also did not apply the Sharia laws for all, and they respected the sentiments of their subjects. These British-sponsored accounts of history argued that Muslim rulers had enslaved India and now the British had come to end the misrule of Muslim kings. Such an account became a convenient tool in the hands of Hindu communalists, the Hindu Mahsabha and the RSS, to play their part of divisive politics amongst masses. The Muslim League turned it around to say that Muslim rulers were glorious and great. The communal interpretation of history is at the core of communalisation. The communal historiography was aimed at propagating that, 'Indian rulers have always been ruled by cruel dictators. In comparison, British rule was the rule of law. The Muslim rulers enslaved Hindus and committed awful atrocities on them; British rulers, on the other hand, rescued the Hindus from the misrule of Muslims, for which Hindus should remain ever grateful to the British and give them full support and that Hindus and Muslims were always divided and at each other's throat and they can never live peacefully with each other in the absence of third party---the British' (Gadkari, p 129). Elliot and Dawson, authors of History of India as told by its own Historians (1849) wrote about the aim of publishing their book: It was to make out native subjects more sensible of the immense advantages accruing to them under the mildness and equity of our rule. (Quoted in Gadkari, p 129.)

The concepts of nationalism promoted by Muslim and Hindu communalists sought continuity from the rule of Muslim and Hindu kings respectively. The way British presented history came in handy for the communalists to legitimise their versions of the past. This version was presented with their contemporary political project. The communal historiographers took over from the British-introduced history books and strengthened the divisive interpretation of the past. 'Communal historiography... drew sustenance from interpretation and selective appropriation of history, and communalist historians were cunningly selective and crudely misleading. Holding the strong view that Hindus and Muslims were distinct sociopolitical entities and were not integrated into cohesive units at any level, communal Hindus and Muslims did not form cohesive units by themselves either' (Udaykumar, 2001, p8).

As such, communal politics uses communal historiography as a starting point of its journey.

As seen in India, 'With partition and accompanying carnage, communalism was broadened from historical interpretation to the larger political and ideological site. Thus communalism becomes, "a consciousness which draws on a supposed religious identity and uses this as a basis for an ideology" and political action' (Romila Thapar, 1989, p 209). In a way this distorted history set into motion a long journey of fear, passion, prejudice and bigotry.

This communalisation of minds was the fertile soil on which the communalists could plant their narrow agenda of Muslim Nation and Hindu Nation. Another British historian, TW Holderness, in his book Peoples and Problems of India mooted the idea that Hindus and Muslims regard themselves as separate nations. This book came out in 1923 and in the same year Savarkar came out with his book, Hindutva or Who is a Hindu? where the same formulation was presented in a different way.

Partition of Bengal

At the ground level on the political chessboard, Lord Curzon, the then Viceroy of India, partitioned Bengal (1905) with communal motivation and this was probably the first concrete experiment in communalising politics in a bigger measure. Curzon went on to declare that this is an attempt to invest in the Mussalmans of Eastern Bengal. Just a year later (1906), the delegation of Muslim landlords and Nawabs was received by the Viceroy, where he declared these Muslim elite to be the representatives of the entire Muslim community in India. The delegation went to ask for separate electorate for Muslims, and these separate electorates introduced later acted as the trigger to polarise the nation along religious lines. Many a members of this delegation were also part of the United India Patriotic Association. The Indian National Congress was critical of the British policy and in response, this association pledged to enhance the loyalty of the people to the British crown.

Thus, then Viceroy, Minto subtly encouraged Muslim communalism, and later the same delegation members went on to form the Muslim League. As pointed out earlier, Lady Minto in her communication took pride in what the Lord had done. She commented that what has happened (the receiving of delegation etc) will pull back sixty million people from joining the ranks of seditious opposition, meaning the rising national movement. This divisive thinking was percolated among Indians through the British school books and through the Muslim League at the political level, by Hindu Mahasabha through its actions and most strongly by the RSS through its shakha bauddhiks, which began from 1925. These organisations all performed the function of 'doctoring of mass consciousness'.

This gave rise to what is known as a 'social common sense', a hatred against the 'other' religious community, which in turn, formed the base for communal violence in time to come. The instigation of communal violence by communal organisations was one of the major factors due to which Mahatma Gandhi had to keep quiet when the decision of partition was accepted. He was totally opposed to the idea of partition, but communal violence made him feel that if partition can prevent the bloodshed so be it.

Political Dynamics of Partition

Lord Curzon, in 1905, partitioned Bengal into the Muslim majority territory of East Bengal and the Hindu majority territory of West Bengal. The British claimed this was done from the point of view of administrative convenience. This move was vehemently opposed by the Hindu communalists and even the Congress. To protect their interests, Muslims pressed for separate electorate, which was agreed to by the British. Meanwhile, the Muslim elite formed the Muslim League in December 1906 to advance the claims of Muslims vis-a-vis other communities. Similarly the Punjab Hindu Sabha in 1909 and Hindu Mahasabha were formed in 1915 with similar goals for the Hindus.

In 1919, the Montegue-Chelmsford reforms introduced a two-tier administration in India: the subjects being divided into transferable and non-transferable ones. The transferable subjects were given to the Indians. Muslims wanted to fight the council elections, in collaboration with the Congress but the Congress party turned down this proposal. Turkey's entry into the war (the First World War) on Germany's side turned the Indian Muslims away from the British. Lokmanya Tilak took advantage of this fact and shepherded the Muslim leaders into the Congress camp. After the Khilafat movement, which attracted a sizeable number of Muslims into the anti-British struggle, Gandhi's 'Non-Cooperation (with British)' call followed. However, differences over reservations for council seats and other political differences led to severe communal riots in early 1920s. There was an attempt at rapprochement by Azad and Anasari but Lala Lajpat Rai wrote a series of 13 articles in *The Tribune*, demanding partition of Bengal and Punjab. He argued that Hindus and Muslims can't live together. Lord Curzon and Lajpat Rai were, therefore, the two people who mothered the partition of India.

The next major hurdle, which impacted separatism, was the effort to draw up the Indian Constitution in the wake of the Simon Commission. Muslim leaders asked for a separate Sind Province, parity of North-West Frontier Province (NWFP) with the other States, one-third representation for Muslims in the central legislature and proportional representation in the Punjab and Bengal assemblies. The Congress proposals came in the form of a report, the Motilal Nehru Report, which had recommended India to be a federation, based on linguistic provinces, provincial autonomy, elections based on joint electorates and seats in central and provincial legislatures reserved for minorities in proportion to their population. This report accepted the initial demands of the Muslims: Separate Sind Province and reforms in NWFP.

At this point, Jinnah agreed to withdraw the demand for a separate electorate, if other demands were accepted. But even the two demands which the Nehru Committee had accepted were withdrawn under pressure from the Hindu Mahasabha and other Hindu communal leaders within the Congress. Jinnah was dejected by the rejection of the Muslim demand and said, 'The Mussalman should be made to feel that they are secure and safeguarded against any act of oppression on the part of the majority and that they need not feel that during transitional stage towards fullest development of a national government, the majority would be in a position to oppress and tyrannise the minority, as majorities are prone to do in other countries' (Mitra,1927, p37).

Jinnah's basic assumption that Muslim League represents all Muslims was a faulty one. As per this theory he wanted to ensure one-third representation, for just 25% of the Muslim population, to be accepted by the committee. This, according to him, was to ensure that no legislation can be passed which is against Muslim interest, since a two-third majority is needed to pass the major legislations.

And so, the real issues, which made the 'divide', were those of the 'elites' of the Hindu and Muslim side. The demands Jinnah was putting forward had to do with the interests of Muslim landlords and traders. Jinnah expanded the first four demands into fourteen demands. This was a severe setback to Hindu-Muslim unity.

Aga Khan, the leader of Muslim delegation at the Round Table Conferences (1931-32), provides a detailed account of the negotiations. He outlines the tragic developments whereby the efforts of Mahatma Gandhi to strike a compromise with Muslim leaders was foiled by Hindu leaders like BS Munje and Madan Mohan Malaviya. According to Sir Tcg Bahadur Sapru, thc Hindus were responsible for failure of these negotiations. Sir Sapru calls this the 'blackest chapter' of the British Indian rule. As an outcome of this Round Table Conference, Sir Ramsay MacDonald declared a 'Communal Award', which had provision for separate electorates for Muslims and Dalits. Neither supported nor opposed it, the Congress did not take any position on this, ie it remained neutral to this award.

MacDonald's Communal Award of 1932 was the next major step in the Hindu-Muslim divide in India. This award bolstered the communal divide. The Congress failed to oppose the award at this crucial juncture. Later in 1939, Congress told the British that they will not join the war (the Second World War) efforts until they were guaranteed freedom. In 1940, Jinnah demanded Pakistan at the Lahore Muslim League convention.

Increasing Distrust

The 1937 assembly elections were a major event, which raised a 'permanent' bogey in Hindu-Muslim relations. Jinnah proposed a joint front of Muslim League and the Congress, who would contest the elections. The Congress rejected it since the Congress wanted land reforms while the Muslim League comprised landlords totally opposed to land reforms. The result was a severe defeat for the Muslim League candidates. After the elections, the UP Muslim League offered to cooperate. It wanted to join the ministry. The Congress turned down this proposal on a similar pretext. This marks another watershed in the politics which led to the formation of Pakistan.

Political observer and commentator Kuldip Nayar points out that, '1937 was a watershed year for Hindu-Muslim relationship. From then on, the differences, which were earlier based on prejudice and social attitudes between two communities began to be institutionalised...(1996)'.

Nehru had his reasons to turn down the League's offer of cooperation, as he was keen to introduce land reforms in UP. If the Muslim League had joined the ministry, the reforms would have been hampered. Maulana Abul Kalam (1998, 174, India Wins Freedom) provides a detailed account of Gandhi's initiative to form a coalition government and Nehru-Patel's counter efforts, which resulted in failure of this joint endeavor. This was one more blow to Jinnah's politics for preserving the interests of the Muslim elite. From this point on, Jinnah felt betrayed and said that the Congress leadership could not be trusted.

Similarly, differences in the perception of interests and the future led the Congress to reject the Cripps Committee proposal for a semi-autonomous federal state. Interestingly, the Muslim League wanted to accept the proposal. At the end of the Second World War, when the Cripps-led 'Cabinet Mission' landed in India, its proposals were acceptable to both parties. The turning point and the setback in negotiations were soon to come. The Cabinet Mission planned to give autonomy to all the States and retain defence, foreign affairs, communication and currency with the central government; that is the British government.

The Congress party, after its initial acceptance of the Cabinet Mission Plan, retracted its position. At this point, Nehru had taken over from Maulana Azad as Congress President. Nehru declared that the 'Constituent Assembly' to be formed under the Cabinet Mission Plan would be the final authority and it may reject the 'autonomous States' and any other proposal of the Cabinet Mission Plan. Jinnah was taken aback and said he could not trust the Congress as it might go back on all the promises, once the British exited the country. Therefore, he took the stand that his demand was Pakistan, nothing more, nothing less. This led to the partition of the country. Maulana Azad was opposed to the partition. Gandhi opposed the partition too but was busy dousing the vitriolic fire of communal violence. For him, the partition was a temporary phenomenon, which would soon be undone.

The British were shuffling and dealing the cards with immaculate precision. They were keen to back 'Project Partition' and created the situations due to which the events eventually moved in the direction of partition. The efforts of the British administration at the political level were to encourage partition and overlook the option of keeping India united.

Administrative Roots of Pakistan Formation

With Mountbatten replacing Lord Wavell as Viceroy, he was better empowered. The dice was rolled. Mountbatten came to the conclusion that partition was the only way out. There were other considerations for Mountbatten's decision. This pertained to the future British interests in the area. The British calculation at this time was that an undivided India under the leadership of the Congress party would not let Britain continue with its military base in the area. Realpolitik dictated the happenings on world stage. USSR was proving to be a military threat, Mao Tse Tung was rising in China and a section of the Congress leadership was enamoured by socialism. Under such circumstances, the UK-USA were sure that India would not ally with them in their global designs of countering Socialism-USSR militarily and in continuing their oil plunder in the Middle East.

Here comes the Radcliff Line, which runs adjacent to Iraq,

Afghanistan and Sinkiang. British diplomats had the job cut out for them, to make Jinnah accept moth-eaten Pakistan and to make the Congress leadership accept the partition (http://www.boloji.com/analysis2/0478.htm).

The imperialist plan was immaculate. And in times to come, Pakistan, where Jinnah wanted to have religious freedom, was converted into a land ruled by mullahs, the military and the American Ambassador. Jinnah was carried away by his self-importance and yielded to the feudal clique of the Muslim League, to join it and advocate its case. He regarded the Muslim elite as the Muslim community. This was far from true. The poor, low caste Muslims did not want Pakistan, nor an Islamic state, nor did they support the Muslim League. This was proven time and time again through their participation in the Indian national movement and through election results in India, especially after partition in a country which is home to 172 million Muslims.

As a matter of fact, after the Lahore Muslim League (1940) resolution which had demanded Pakistan, there was a wide uproar amongst the poor Muslims who opposed the idea of Pakistan. Also the major Muslim seminaries of Barelvi and Deoband backed the idea of a composite Indian nationalism, which was the goal of the national movement. Jinnah himself was earlier a part of the Indian National Congress. He started to drift away from national movement and Congress after Gandhi wanted to involve common people in anti-British struggle. With his giving the call of 'Non-cooperation' with the British, Jinnah felt disturbed. Jinnah was essentially a Constitutionalist who thought that politics is the preserve of the elite and common people joining it will result in severe disturbances.

Jinnah, as is known, had a secular soul. He wanted to operate within the confines of the law. He was opposed to the involvement of the masses with the anti-British movement. Therefore, LK Advani and Jaswant Singh are right when they call him secular. However, the problem is, Jinnah was appointed the supreme leader of a feudal group, the Muslim League, which was totally communal. So one can say, Jinnah was a 'secular soul in a communal body'.

Historians speculate that the Cabinet Mission Plan, which was based on Maulana Azad's proposal, would have prevented the partition of India, but the Congress leadership retracted on it. True, the Congress had accepted this plan in the beginning. According to this plan, India was to be a federal state. All the powers were to be with the provinces except those related to defence, communication, currency and external affairs. The Congress, mainly Nehru and Patel, realised that such an arrangement would not let them have planned development and political power. So they backed out from this arrangement. Here, the long-term goals of different leaders were different. The Congress was looking forward to social transformation, industrialisation, while the Muslim League was satisfied with the status quo of landlordism.

Later, more differences cropped up over the nature of the Constituent Assembly and the autonomy of provinces. Jinnah was for autonomy of States whereas Nehru-Patel favoured a strong centre. Fearful of the dominant majority of the Hindus, Jinnah wanted to ensure a share for the Muslim elite. His stubbornness began with the rejection of proposals from the Motilal Nehru Committee, his wish to fight the elections jointly and then share power in the assemblies, which the Congress rejected. According to Maulana Abul Kalam Azad (India Wins Freedom), the Congress leaders made a tactical mistake by refusing to share power with the Muslim League after the 1937 elections in UP. This strengthened the prevalent communal, 'Two Nation Theory' and led to the vivisection of the country.

Congress had its own reasons to spurn Jinnah's demands. To begin with, the Congress party regarded itself as the representative of all sections of society; in fact it had a fair representation of Muslims as well. Amongst all the haze and confusion, Mahatma Gandhi was the one to press for coalition governments but he was not taken seriously on this issue. We should note that prominent Ulema of the subcontinent like Maulana Husain Ahmad Madani, Maulana Hifazur Rahman and others strongly opposed Jinnah and his 'Two Nation Theory'. The Ulama stood for a composite nationalism, they justified creation of a secular, composite nationalism in India. This (difference over the Constituent Assembly and autonomy of provinces) was the last blow to the possibility of an united India.

This led Jinnah to accept a truncated Pakistan and Nehru-Patel to opt for partition rather than a weak federal state.

Trauma of India's Partition

The partition trajectory went to a higher pitch with controversies that came up in the wake of the formation of the Nehru Committee. Jinnah submitted a 14-point charter which was formulated around 1929. This mostly related to secular demands (there was nothing in the charter about religious freedom for Muslims): effective representation of Muslims in legislatures, separation of Sindh from Bombay province, continuation of separate electorate etc. It asked for one-third representation for 25% Muslims, to prevent approval of changes in statutes by the Hindu majority.

The Nehru Committee rejected one-third representation. Muslims offered to give up their demand for separate electorate if the following are granted:

1. Sind to be a separate province.
2. Reforms in North West Frontier Province.
3. In Bengal and Punjab, per cent of representation as per population.
4. One-third representation in the legislatures.

Though these were demands mainly of elite Muslims, they were accepted by the Nehru committee. Later, under pressure of the Hindu Mahasabha, the Congress turned down these demands.

Around 1930, Lala Lajpat Rai demanded partition of the country in a letter to Gandhi. During the colonial period, there was decline of Muslim landlords and adverse representation of Muslims in jobs, except in UP. There occurred rise of traders (mainly Hindus) and part of colonial commercial bourgeoisie transformed into India's first industrial bourgeoisie.

In 1937 elections, the Congress won majority in many States and formed governments. It rejected Jinnah's demand for incorporation of Muslim representatives in its ministries. In 1937, at the Hindu Mahasabha convention, Bhai Parmanand said, 'Mr Jinnah argues, there are two nations in the country (Hindus and Muslims), he is right. Congress theory of building a common nationality falls to the ground. There are only two options (1) Partition of country (2) allow Muslim state to grow in the present state'.

The Congress leadership had only two options:

1. Strong centre with partition
2. Loose federation without partition.

They opted for 1, despite Gandhi's opposition to this.

In the Ajmer session, the Hindu Mahasabha in 1937 demanded the partition of the country. Most of the Muslim elite were for the same. The Muslim elite, through the Muslim League, had demanded higher representation with an eye to more government privileges and when these were rejected they became firm in their demand for Pakistan, hoping this will give them unlimited power and will also avoid the competition from Hindu elite.

Trajectory of events leading to formation of Pakistan

Muslim Communal Politics	Hindu Communal Politics
1860: Sir Syed Ahmed articulates the need for modern education and jobs for Muslim	Hindu Zamindars and elite demand a share of seats in legislature and call for cow slaughter ban
1906: Formation of Muslim League, fearing Hindu majority. Was mainly a body of landlords and Princes	1909: Formation of the Punjab Hindu Sabha by Hindu elite, landlords and Rajas (Princes)
	1915: Hindu Mahasabha formed
	1924: Lala Lajpat Rai wrote13 articles in The Tribune saying that Hindus and Muslims can't live together, Bengal and Punjab should be partitioned. 1925:Rashtriya Swayam Sevak Sangh formed
Nehru Committee Report, 1927	

4-point demand by Muslim League, rejection of demands by Nehru Committee	Nehru Committee under pressure from Hindu Mahasabha rejected the 4-point demand of the Muslim League. This formed the first base of demand for Pakistan
Poet Iqbal demands separate homeland for Muslims in North West	1930: Lala Lajpat Rai, in a letter to Mahatma Gandhi, demands the partition of the country
Chaudhary Rahmat Ali coins the word Pakistan. P for Punjab, A for Afghans (Pathans), K for Kashmir, S for Sind and Stan the Persian suffix meaning land	1933: Bhai Parmanand, President Hindu Mahasabha, calls for cooperation with the British to settle scores with Muslims
1932: Macdonald's Communal Award	1937: Hindu Mahasabha: Ajmer session resolution says Hindus and Muslims are two separate nations
1937: The Muslim demand of fighting elections jointly and then participating in the government is rejected by the Congress. Jinnah's Two Nation Theory takes shape	
	1938: Bhai Parmanand 'Mr Jinnah argues that there are two nations in the country... If Mr Jinnah is right and I believe he is, then the Congress theory of building common nationality falls to ground. This situation has got two solutions. One is the partition of country into two and the other to allow the Muslim state to grow within the Hindu State'
Cabinet Mission Plans (1945) autonomy of States: Unacceptable to Congress. Nehru's stand that forthcoming Constituent Assembly can change the earlier agreements comes as the final blow to unity efforts. Impasse. Partition proposed by Mountbatten. Acceptance by both Congress and Muslim League	

Muslims were 25% of the population. As the franchise was based on property holding or education, only 10% of these were eligible to vote. From amongst these, only 60% voted for the Muslim League. When the resolution for creation of Pakistan was passed in the Lahore convention of the Muslim League, many poor Muslims took out a procession condemning this resolution demanding Pakistan.

Causes of Growth of Communalism in India

The emergence of Muslim League and Hindu Mahasabha had its roots in multiple factors. Since it was a colonial economy, the elimination of the feudal system could not take place. The feudal elements, along with feudal values, continued and they expressed their political demands through communal politics. This, in turn, can be understood through following points, which contributed to rise of communal streams in Indian politics.

1. Slow development of economy, persistence of feudal set up.
2. Competition between Hindu and Muslim elite.
3. Weak mercantile bourgeoisie vis-a-vis feudal lords.
4. British policy of divide and rule.
5. Muslim League: representatives only of Muslim elites. Political leadership like Khan Abdul Gaffar Khan, Hakim Ajmal Khan, Dr Ansari, Maulana Abul Kalam Azad stood for secular nationalism, Hindu Muslim unity and anti-British struggles. Maulana Hussain Ahmed Madani said: 'These days nations are based on geographical boundaries and not on religion: France, America etc are examples of that.'
6. Hindu Mahasabha had initially Rajas and Hindu landlords. Later RSS was started by Brahmin elite, upper caste supported by landlords, Rajas and traders.

The Two Nation Theory

Two Nation theory means the argument that there are two nations in India, one of Hindus and another of Muslims. This concept of nationalism was based on religion of the community. The Two Nation theory was initially put forward by both kinds of communalists, the Hindu Mahasabha, the RSS and the Muslim

League. While the communalists worked on that right from the beginning, its articulation came with Vinayak Damodar Savarkar's *Hindutva or Who is a Hindu?* Here one sees a clear formulation that India is a Hindu nation. That, nation states are based on religion. This was totally in opposition to the undercurrent of the national movement, which regarded that all people living in this region are Indians, and that religion is not the basis of the Indian nation state. Similarly, elite Muslim intellectuals came up with the concept that Muslims are a separate nation. Thus, three concepts of nationalism prevailed at a single point in time. The national movement, the Socialist streams and Ambedkar argued that India is a nation in the making, while Muslim communalists asserted they are a Muslim nation ever since Mohammed Bin-Kasim invaded Sindh and ruled there. Hindu communalists claimed that India is a Hindu nation from time immemorial. So Hindu and Muslim communalists were united in their understanding that religion is the basis of a nation state. The difference and antagonism came at the level of power. Hindu communalists asserted that the country belongs to Hindus, Muslims should either leave or remain subservient to Hindus. Muslim communalists said that since Hindus are dominant, so the only way to preserve the rights of Muslims is to have a separate Muslim state (land), Pakistan. Accordingly, the political streams from Group A (above), Bhagat Singh, Ambedkar and Gandhi saw India as a nation in the making, a modern nation state to be based on the values of democracy, secularism. The political streams coming from Group B (Muslim League, Hindu Mahasabha, RSS) asserted that India is exclusively a Hindu nation or that a Muslim nation is present here.

Post-partition

After partition, the Muslim elite, bureaucrats, businessman, rich landlords left for Pakistan. The larger section of Muslims, who remained behind were not the ones' asking for Pakistan. These poor, landless, self-employed artisans etc had never been part of the demand for Pakistan. Due to partition, the Muslim community in India shrunk in size. It got subdued and communal forces started blaming them for the partition.

On the other hand, in due course, West Pakistan's dominant elite started exploiting East Pakistan economically, started dominating it politically and started imposing its concept of cultural nationalism (Urdu, Muslim, Pakistan) on Pakistan as a whole. This led to the people from East Pakistan to separate from Pakistan to form Bangladesh, with assistance from the Indian army. The elite Muslims who went to Pakistan, initially got good treatment there, but later the Muslims going from India to Pakistan were humiliated, given stepmotherly treatment. They were called Mohajirs and are living a subdued life in ghettoes.

In Pakistan while Jinnah talked of separation of state and religion, most of the leadership around him thought otherwise. After Jinnah's death, the communal elements started becoming stronger. The military and mullahs became stronger politically and Pakistan unfortunately came under the grip of these undemocratic elements. With Zia ul Haq grabbing power, Maulana Maududi's fundamentalist ideology started ruling the roost. The power equation in Pakistan came to be America, Allah (mullah) and Army. It is a matter of great relief that democracy is trying to stabilise there during the last few years.

British Interests and Partition

No doubt the Cabinet Mission Plan could have prevented partition, but it is debatable whether it would not have sown fissiparous tendencies amongst the princely States and the States where Muslim League was in majority. Pakistan was supported to the hilt by the US on the Kashmir issue; the idea was that US strategic interests were safe with this arrangement. It is a matter of great relief that Pakistan is struggling to come out from the vice-like grip of its Army, but can it shed its client state status vis a vis US? This is the million rupee question. The people of Pakistan have been big victim of imperialist designs all through, while Pakistan's military has been having all the green pastures for itself.

In partitioning India, colonialists reaped rich harvest at the cost of the people of the subcontinent; millions dead, a single entity India, divided into Pakistan, India and Bangladesh. These countries keep on spending a major part of their budgets in investing in armaments and fattening of their armed forces, something which could have been meaningfully invested for the growth and development of the respective region. We need to wake up from the blame game and see the real culprit. Gandhi summarised the British goals in India very well, 'It is preposterous to suggest that... [Hindus and Muslims] cannot live together amicably because the Hindus believe in Ahimsa and the Mohamadans do not. Those thoughts are put into our minds by selfish and false religious teachers. The English put finishing touches to it. They have a habit of writing history; they pretend to study the manners and customs of all people....They write about their own research in most laudatory terms and hypnotise us into believing them. We, in our ignorance, fall at their feet' (Gandhi, 1938 p 52).

Gandhi, Maulana Azad and Partition

Mahatma Gandhi entered the Indian political scenario in the 1920s and galvanised the socio-political dynamics of the country. His basic and main concern was to gain independence of the country from the clutches of colonial powers. Even before his entry into Indian politics, the Muslim League, the Hindu Mahasabha and Congress were active, each with its own different agenda. There was no mass movement, which could involve all the people to oppose the British role. Politics was restricted to the politics of the elite, in the form of petitions etc.

Gandhi evoked the imagination of the masses by bringing them into the freedom struggle. For this purpose, initially he used religious symbolisms and religious issues to appeal to the people. Since the political forces were fragmented, he wanted to channelise them into a single political force. For this, he used the Khilafat to mobilise Muslims, and anti-untouchability campaigns to mobilise sections of the Hindu population. His religious tolerance was extreme and though a devout Hindu himself, he did respect other religions equally. That Gandhi loved Muslims more is a myth propagated by Hindu communalists who say this country belongs to Hindus, and that the other communities should remain subservient to Hindus. In contrast to this, Gandhi advocated equal rights to people, irrespective of their religious affiliations. He dealt with different types of Muslim leaderships differently.

While he wanted to negotiate with leaders of the Muslim League, his politics also brought to the fore Muslim leaders like Maulana Abul Kalam Azad, Khan Abdul Gaffar Khan and Rafi Ahmed Kidwai who joined the secular political movement and participated wholeheartedly in anti-British struggles. Hindu communalists hated both, negotiations with the Muslim League and bringing the Muslim masses into the mainstream of India's socio-political movement. It was Gandhian leadership which drew out the poor, majority of the country, irrespective of their religion, into the anti-British struggle. We have seen that the formation of Pakistan was due to pulls and pressures of communalists, due to failure of negotiations between the Muslim League and the Congress, and because of the role of British rulers and pulls of Hindu communalism. Many a times, Gandhi was for compromises which could have restored the faith of the Muslim League in the majority party, ie the Congress. That's why he wanted the Congress to incorporate Muslim League members in the State ministries in 1937. Contrary to this, since all negotiations failed and both kinds of elites saw the emergence of separate state being better for 'their' respective interests, the demand for Pakistan was conceded.

Not just satisfied with criticism, a section of Hindu communalists, votaries of Hindu Rashtra, conspired to kill the Mahatma. They hated him for his genuine secularism and his murder was prompted by his principled stand of fair distribution of state treasury and parting with Rs 55 crore, which was Pakistan's share of the treasury. Hindu communalists wanted to subjugate the Muslims on the ground that this is a Hindu Rashtra, while Gandhi, believing in secular principles, was treating Muslims on par. This was unacceptable to the Hindu communal forces and hence the criticism and the falsehood built around this Rs 55 crore. Even today, Hindu communalists keep spreading the lie that it was Gandhi because of whom Muslims succeeded in getting Pakistan. It was the Savarkars and Golwalkars who propagated the two nation theory.

Maulan Abul Kalam Azad was not only a Muslim scholar of repute but a member of the central committee of the Congress and its President during early 1940s. He was totally against the idea of partition of India, as he felt that it will not only harm India as a whole but Muslims will be the bigger looser in the whole exercise. He felt Muslims who will remain in India will be much more fragmented and weaker in number. He was for a structure of a federal state with full autonomy for provinces; he fully went with the Cabinet Mission report, which had this opinion. 'Hence Maulana Abul Kalam Azad, who knew his Islam and his history better than others, spoke of a notable event in history, the fusion of the Islamic and Hindu cultural currents, and eleven hundred years of common history. This joint wealth, according to him, was the heritage of common nationality' (Mushirul Hasan, *Legacy of a Divided Nation,* p 11, OUP, 2001).

The Maulana writes, 'I am proud of being an Indian, I am part of the indivisible unity that is Indian nationality. I am indispensable to this noble edifice and without me this splendid structure of India is incomplete. I am an essential element which has gone to build India. I can never surrender this claim' (Azad, Ramgarh, March 1940). He held Nehru and Patel responsible for partition as, according to him, Nehru's not taking two Muslim League members in the UP cabinet after the elections of 1937, and his going back on the Cabinet Mission Plan after he took over as President from Maulana Azad, left the Muslim League in the lurch and they became more disgruntled. With these developments, Jinnah became obstinate and declared that he will not compromise with anything short of Pakistan. Maualana Azad reluctantly gave into the decision of Pakistan as an inevitability, which he could not prevent.(http://www.csss-isla.com/archive/archive.php?article=2009/sep1_sep15.htm)

Azad still faced the partition tragedy with dignity. Kenneth Cragg points out, 'He could envisage Hinduism and Islam not of sectarian belligerence but of confident partnership with other cultural and religious entities' (Kenneth Cragg, 1986, p 29).

Jinnah, Nehru, Patel

Apportioning the blame of partition on these leaders has been diverse. The Muslim League and many other leaders put the blame on Nehru and Patel, while a large section of the Congress, and Hindu communalists in particular, held Jinnah to be the sole person responsible for creation of Pakistan.

The personality of Jinnah is very complex. 'The only thing Muslim about Jinnah was his parents' religion. He drank, ate pork, religiously shaved his beard each morning and just as religiously avoided mosque each Friday. God and Koran had no place in the Jinnah's vision of the World' (Lal Khan, 2007, p 66). He was a British-educated barrister, seeped in values of Hindu-Muslim unity and Indian nationalism. Jinnah returned to India as a 'secular liberal nationalist'. He was a follower of Dada Bhai Nowrojee. He was opposed to separate electorate and kept aloof from the Muslim League for some time. Many a factor in his life led him gradually to the arms of the Muslim League, and his brilliance as a lawyer made him the leader of the Muslim League, to the extent that he soon became the sole spokesman of the Muslim communal voice. This drift was gradual, the main shift coming in 1919 when he opposed the non-cooperation movement and the participation of masses in the national movement.

He was a Constitutionalist and was opposed to the participation of masses in politics. This is what led him to drift away from the Gandhi-led national movement and in due course he gravitated towards the Muslim League. Opposed to the mass movements of 1919-1920, he tilted towards Muslim communal politics and became much more opposed to the Congress after the 1930's mass movement led by the Congress. As a brilliant lawyer he took up the case of 'Muslims', and as it turned out, it was mainly the cause of the Muslim elite, not of the Muslim masses. His differences with the Congress started getting sharper and intense after Motilal Nehru rejected his demands (1928). Later, after the Congress refused to include Muslim League members in the UP cabinet and after Nehru went back from the promise of adhering to the Cabinet Mission Plan, Jinnah became adamant that he will compromise with nothing less than Pakistan. While being a non-practicing Muslim, he was espousing the cause of Muslim communalism and the logic of this led him to advocate the two nation theory and demand Pakistan.

It is important to note that while evaluating Jinnah, his changing stance over a period of time is crucial in grasping his politics. Starting from when he was an ambassador of Hindu-Muslim unity, to becoming the spokesman of Pakistan, there have been various stages. Prior to 1940, one can find in his speeches and writings, a repeated mention of Hindu-Muslim amity, cultural pluralism and secularity, while being strongly critical of the Congress and its leadership. '...he sharply denounced the Congress leaders, accusing them of alienating Muslims through "Hindu" policies, and creating class bitterness and communal war, and strengthening the imperialist hold' (Sharifuddin Pirzada, (ed) 1970, 268).

In due course, he went on to cultivate the image of a 20th Century Muslim Messiah, out to liberate his community from the shackles of 'Hindu tyranny'. Now he focused more on the assertion that Muslims formed a separate nation, by any standard definition and so they must secure their homeland. The responsibility of getting for Muslims their state was put on educated Muslims. 'Unless you get this into your blood', they were told emphatically, 'unless you are willing to take your coats off and willing to sacrifice all, unless you can work selflessly, earnestly and sincerely for your people, you will never realise your dream' (Pirzada Foundation, Vol 2 p338, 339).

What is the role of Jinnah in bringing about partition process to its fruition? He contributed by '...his forceful articulation of two nation theory and his success in mobilising people in such large numbers and to such great effect. For those confronted with and troubled by partition's bitter legacy, the critical and unresolved issue is how the Quiad (leader) and his lieutenants came up with and effectively deployed a powerful symbol to galvanise Muslims and create in them the urge to join the crusade for a separate homeland. How their goals were achieved in so short a time requires examination' (Hasan, 2001, p 55).

Jinnah's major flaw was to be opposed to participation of masses in the freedom movement and to regard Muslim League as representative of Muslim community, despite the fact that it was founded by Muslim aristocracy and was full of feudal lords. This is what the trouble was, even after the birth of Pakistan. It was a country with sharp class difference.

There are some similarities between the transitions of Jinnah from a secular nationalist to leader of the Muslim League with Vinayak Damodar Savarkar, the leader of Hindu communalism. Savarkar was an anti-British revolutionary in the initial stages of his political life. He was jailed for such activities. During the jail tenure, he developed his political ideology of Hindutva, which gave ideological foundation for Hindu communalism. He tendered an apology to the British, got released from jail and also turned from an anti-British revolutionary to a Hindu communalist, servile to British designs in the subcontinent.

At the level of the political-administrative trajectory of partition, Nehru's statement on the Cabinet Mission Plan was a turning point. The Federal character of India, which was accepted by the Muslim League and the Congress both, was put under cloud by Nehru when he became President of the Congress in 1946. He said that they are going with an open mind on the issue, ie. the plan of the Cabinet Mission was not sacrosanct (final) as far as the Congress was concerned. This is what made Jinnah assert that he will not compromise with anything short of Pakistan. Nehru never regarded communalists as representative of the respective religious communities. He had opposed electoral alliance with the Muslim League in 1937, he had turned down the proposal of the Muslim League to have two of their representatives in UP ministry. Idealist as he was, Nehru was not willing to grant any legitimacy to communalists as he also had the vision of land reforms, while the Muslim League and the Hindu Mahasabha were dominated by landlords.

In response to the developments of 1946, Mountbatten suggested partition of India, very much in tune with British designs of continuing their strategic interests in the region. From amongst Indian leaders, Sardar Patel was the first to accept that proposal as formulated by Lord Mountbatten. Sardar Patel 'was convinced that he could not work with the Muslim League' (Lal Khan, *Partition*, p69). Maulana Abul Kalam Azad writes, '...Patel said, whether we like it or not there are two nations in India. He was now convinced that Hindus and Muslims could not be united into one nation. It was better to have one clean fight and separate than have bickering every day. I was surprised that Patel was now an even greater supporter of the two nation theory than Jinnah' (Quoted in Lal Khan p 69).

Nehru and Patel were not only focusing on getting rid of British rule but wanted to shape an India which was strong and which went in for land reforms etc. This was the precise reason as to why Nehru opposed the demand of the Muslim League members being taken in the UP cabinet. And since the Cabinet Mission Plan talked of autonomy of provinces at the cost of a strong center, Nehru and Patel conceded partition to see a strong center where development and centralised planning can be at the core of government policies.

References

Achin Vanaik, *Communalism Contested,* Sage, New Delhi, 1997.

'Act of Brotherhood of Young Europe', 1783, quoted in Hobsbawm, *The Age of Revolution 1789-1848*, p 164.

Asghar Ali Engineer, *Medieval History and Communalism*, CSSS Mumbai 1998, p 5.

Arvind Panagariya, Some Questions are best buried, *Times of India,* Mumbai, 31, Oct 2009.

Ashok Chausalkar, Communalism, and History, Text books in Maharashtra, *Towards Secular India*, Jan 1995, 66.

Bipan Chandra, *Modern India*, NCERT, 1990, page 271.

Bipan Chandra, *Communalism in Modern India*, p 548.

Bipan Chandra, *History of Modern India*, Orient Blackswan, Delhi 2009, pg 131.

Bipan Chandra, *Indian National Movement*, Har Anand, 2010, p11.

Hobsbawm, *The Age of Revolution* 1789-1848, Rupa, Calcutta, 1992, p 37.

Faiz, in VG Kienan (Ed.), *Poems by Faiz*, (London, 1971) p. 123.

Francis Robinson, p 131, *Indian Political Economy* 1947-1977.

Gopal Das Khosla: *Stern Reckoning*, Quoted by C Subramanyam in *Independence and the pain of Partition.*

Jaswant Singh, quoted in *TOI*, Mumbai August 17, 2009.

Jayant Gadkari, Hindu Muslim Communalism: A Panchnama, Kosambi Memorial Trust Mumbai, 1999, p 54.

Jawaharlal Nehru, Quoted in Bipan Chadra, *Modern India*, NCERT, 1990, page 271.
Jawaharlal Nehru, Speech in Bhopal 9th July 1958, quoted in Mushirul Hasan, *Legacy of a Divided Nation*, OUP, Delhi 2001, pg 100.
Kenneth Cragg, *The Pen and the Faith*, Delhi ISPCK 1986, p 29.
KN Panikkar, in Bipan Chandra, *India's Struggle for Independence,* Penguin, Delhi 1988, page 73.
Lal Khan, *Partition: Can it be Undone*, Aakar, Delhi, 2007, p 66.
MS Golwalkar, 'Bunch of Thoughts', 152, quoted in Bipan Chandra, 1988.
Maulana Abul Kalam Azad, *India Wins Freedom.*
Maulan Abul Kalam Azad, Presidential Address, Indian National Congress, Fifty Third Session, Ramgarh March 1940.
Mehta and Patwardhan, p 43, *The Communal Triangle of India*, Quoted in Gadkari, p90.
NN Mitra (ed), Indian Quarterly Register, Vol I, 1927, 37.
Mohaamad Ali Jinnah, Speech in Constituent Assemble, http://www.pakistani.org/pakistan/legislation/constituent_address_11aug1947.html, accessed on 13 07 2010.
Mohammad Ali Jinnah. Speeches and Writings, ed. Ahmed Jamiluddin, p 567.
Mohandas Karamchand Gandhi, *Hind Swaraj or Indian Home Rule*, Ahmedabad, Navjivan Publishing House, 1938 p 52.
Mushirul Hasan, *India Partitioned: The Other Face of Freedom,* 2005, Roli Books, Delhi.
Mushirul Hasan, *Inventing Boundaries,* OUP Delhi, 2000, p 7.
Mushirul Hasan, *Legacy of a Divided Nation,* p 11, OUP, 2001.
Percival Spear, *A History of India* Volume II, Penguin, 1990, p 170.
Ram Puniyani, *Communal Politics,* Sage, Delhi 2003, p 43.
Romila Thapar, Imagined Religious Communities? 'Ancient History and Modern Search for a Hindu Identity', *Modern Asian Studies* 23/2 (1989) p 209.
S Gopal, *British Policy in India 1858 to 1905*, p 36.
Sharifuddin Pirzada, (ed) *Foundations of Pakistan*, Karachi: National Publishing House, 1970) vol. 2 p 268.
SP Udaykumar, *Handcuffed to History,* Praeger, London, 2001, p.8.
Sumit Sarkar, *History of India,* Macmillan, Delhi, 1996 p 59.
Surendra Rao, review of *Partition of India* by Ian Talbot and Gurupal Singh, Cambridge University Press, *The Hindu* Jan 5 2010.
Urvashi Butalia, *The Other Side of Silence: Voices from Partition of India*, Penguin Delhi 1998, p 10.

Web

http://www.csss-isla.com/archive/archive.php?article=2009/sep1_sep15.htm

http://www.boloji.com/analysis2/0478.htm, accessed on 31st August 2009

http://www.boloji.com/analysis2/0478.htm, accessed on 31st August 2009

http://www.csss-isla.com/archive/archive.php?article=2009/sep1_sep15.htm

Reading List

AA Engineer: *Communalism in India*, Vikas, 1995.

AA Engineer: *Pakistan, Religion, Politics and Society*,CSSS Bombay, March 16, 1996.

HMSeervai, *Legend and Reality*, Emmenem, 1989.

J Anand & Teesta Setalvad, *Communalism Combat*, August 1996.

Kuldip Nayyar: A Tale of two 'Nations', *Outlook*, Oct. 2, 1996.

Maulana Abul Kalam Azad, *India Wins Freedom,* Orient Longman, 1988.

Mushirul Hasan, *India's Partition: Process, Strategy and Mobilization*, OUP, 1998.

Mushirul Hasan, *Inventing Boudaries*, OUP, 2000.

Moin Shakir, 'Dynamics of Muslim Thought', in *Political Thought in Modern India* (Ed: Pantham & Deutsch) Sage 1986.

NN Mitra ed. *Indian Quarterly Register*, 1927, Vol.1.

Percival Spear *A History of India* (vol2), Penguin, 1990.

Rafiq Zakaria,: 'The Truth of Appeasement', in *Indian Muslims,* Ed. Rajkishore (Hindi) Vani Prakashan, 1994. (This article draws heavily from books of HM Seervai and Ayesha Jalal.)

INDO-PAK RELATIONS

A Tale of Two Neighbours

India and Pakistan have been living as uncomfortable neighbours. The attack on Mumbai on 26 November 2008 not only killed a number of innocents, it also put their relations under severe strain. While the terror groups have originated in Pakistan and the Pakistan government has not been able to comply with the request made by India to hand them over to India, the popular opinion in India is becoming very hostile to Pakistan.

After the partition tragedy, the first major war between these neighbours took place on the issue of Kashmir. This resulted in one third of Kashmir becoming 'Azad Kashmir' in the military ruled Pakistan and two-third coming under the control of democratic India, with lakhs of soldiers breathing down the neck of Kashmiri civilians.

The second war, 1965, took place over the boundary issue of Rann of Kutch. The war was inconclusive. With the Pakistani rulers oppressing East Pakistan, the popular rebellion in East Pakistan got crystallized as Mukti Bahini, which with the help of Indian army, succeeded in creating separate Bangladesh in 1971.

While Pakistan slipped into the grips of Army and Maulanas, overseen by the authority of the US, democratic India has been seeing the rise of the Hindu Right. The concept of Hindu nation has been oppressing the minorities in the form of communal violence, insecurity, undermining of their identity and falling in their socio-economic standard. The Indian Muslims have been labelled as being 'loyal to Pakistan' and have been demonised and ghettoised.

The internal and external policies of both these governments and dominant political forces have been vitiating the atmosphere. There have also been positive efforts in the direction, the Shimla Agreement, Vajpayee's bus Yatra, Musharraf's Agra trip etc but matters are in a flux and peace is very elusive at the moment.

Towards Peaceful Indo-Pak Relations

The efforts for peace do need a pursuit of this goal by recourse to Gandhian methods. The values of communal amity, the method of involving broad layers of the people in the process has to be taken up more seriously. It is imperative that we shun violence; war, use of nuclear arms or the threat of these. War is not a solution; it is a problem by itself. While one concedes that the US designs have so far been worsening the scenario, it is also to be noted that local jingoistic and war mongering groups have been adding salt to the injury. What we need is the process of dialogue between all aggrieved parties, strengthening of democracy from grassroots level to the global level and the ability to see the plight of those suffering due to the tension between various countries.

We also need to address the issues related to Kashmir, to ensure that people of Kashmir become part of the process of conflict resolution, We need a reduction in the size of armies, pacts like no war pacts, resolves like 'no use of nuclear weapons' and to open up trade-culture-sports and educational links as much as possible. People-to-people interactions need to be given a shot in the arms and Gandhian attitude of ability to see the other's point of view, while putting forward one's own is crucial to the process.

The South Asian region has been a troubled zone ever since the end of the Second World War. There have been regular and repetitive violence, and a sort of cold indifference towards each other among all the countries in this region, including Myanmar, Bangladesh and Afghanistan. The regions which could have flourished industrially, educationally and economically, are ridden with inter-state disputes over the nagging problem of Kashmir.

Whether it should merge with Pakistan or India has been a source of pain and torture for the Kashmiris. With the onset of the Al Qaeda's activities, terrorism resorted to in the name of Islam, misuse of words like Jihad and Kafir, have affected both India and Pakistan in equal measures. Since the Al Qaeda terror camps were planted by the US on the soil of Pakistan, India feels Pakistan needs to do more to stop the repeated recurrence of dastardly acts of terrorism on Indian soil, while Pakistan herself remains terribly mired in the tragedies heaped on it by Al Qaeda clones.

The hawks on both sides of the divide are having a field day. In India, immediately after the attack on Mumbai on 26th November 2008, Pakistan Murdabad (Death to Pakistan) became the slogan of a section of peace marchers, while Pakistan, feeling helpless under diverse pressures, kept shifting its responses to India's demands and accusations.

What is missing on the ground is the mutual confidence and attempt to see the 'other's' point of view and the whole picture due to which, the 'other' is helpless. Any attempt to recall the Gandhian approach to the issues on hand is equally missing. The ingredients of Gandhi's major approach were to recognise the problem in depth, to see the grievances of the parties affected and to reconcile the problem on the basis of justice and non-violence. Let's see how the Gandhian approache is a must and probably the only way to have peace in the region.

Pakistan

While India began its tryst with destiny through the democratic path, Pakistan had problems in pursuing the democratic path from the very beginning. Mohammad Ali Jinnah, Qaed-e-Azam, the architect of Pakistan did make democratic proclamations in the beginning. His speech in the Pakistan Parliament was a landmark in defining secularism. But as he was surrounded by the landlord, Nawabs and other communal elements, Pakistan soon fell into the clutches of military dictatorship and in due course, the country came to be ruled by three As, Allah (mullah), Army and America. It soon became clear that it is difficult for democracy to be rooted there due to all these elements who play

their vested interests and have slowly converted Pakistan into a hotbed of obscurantism and US base for military and political operations in the subcontinent through military rule.
Military rule began with Field Marshal Ayub Khan, through Yahya Khan, Zia Ul Haq and finally to Pervez Musharraf. Military came to occupy a painfully important place in the polity of Pakistan; mullahs had a field day and America merrily went to militarise the Asian regions, and in that direction, planted the poisonous seeds of Al Qaeda, which is the most visible face of politics in the name of Islam, abusing the identity of Islam.

India: A Contrasting Picture

In India democracy went through various hiccups, and after the initial immaculate leadership of Jawaharlal Nehru, the regional, linguistic, casteist and communal forces started throwing up their ugly agenda. Indira Gandhi also smothered democracy by imposing Emergency in 1975 to quell a movement launched by Jayapraksh Narayan. Jayapraksh Narayan allied with communal forces of the RSS, who practically took over the movement, to plant the poisonous weeds of a divisive agenda in north Indian politics. At the same time, caste elements also came up the dalits and OBCs, deprived from a very long time, today demand justice for their communities. Thus the political chessboard in India started being infiltrated by communal elements and right-wing politics was unfolded through the politics of parties and groups like the BJP, VHP, Samajik Samrasta Manch, Vanvasi Kalyan Ahsram, Rashtra Sevika Samiti and hordes of other similar so-called social and religious organisations attempting to implement their agenda of abolishing democracy and secularism, to create a Hindu Rashtra in the contemporary context of communal fascism. Overall, in the international arena, in general and South Asian affairs in particular, Indira had her own policies, dictated by national interests. Besides this, there has been in operation in India the pro-US agenda of the UPA (alliance led by Congress) governments that followed Indira and the pro-Israel and subservient policies of the NDA (alliance led by BJP) regimes. In the matters of negotiation with each other, these countries have kept various factors in their mind. Lately, especially after the US invasion of Iraq, US has been gradually trying to dump its loyal subservient Pakistan regime, and taking cognizance of India, more than before. Thus diverse factors have played their role in the Indo-Pak relations. India was pursuing the path of nonalignment till the early nineties, when she stopped paying much heed to the values of nonalignment and started tilting towards US.

Al Qaeda was propped up by America during the cold war era, after USSR forces occupied Afghanistan. As US intervention in Vietnam brought a lot of criticism at home and abroad, so the US decided not to send its armies to counter the USSR move. Instead, it encouraged the formation of Al Qaeda through especially set up Madrassas in Pakistan. In these Madrassas, Muslim youth fell prey to the US plan to use Muslim youths to fight the USSR armies. To prepare these youth to fight the USSR army, the plan was to indoctrinate them. The syllabus of these Madrassas was designed in Washington. Here, half truths were cleverly turned into blatant truths to prepare these youth to take up the battle against the Soviet armies in the name of Islam, and as against communism. In this module used in Pakistan Madrassas, the meaning of the term 'Jihad (striving)' was changed to war against non-believers, and 'Kafir (one who is hidden)' to those who are non-Muslims. And a 'Kurbani (sacrifice)' was solicited for the service of Islam, as a reward for this sacrifice, the believing youth were told that after getting killed in this Jihad, they would land up straight in 'Jannat (Heaven)' where 72 virgins will be welcoming each one of them! Osama bin Laden was made the chief of this Al Qaeda, which was richly funded by the US through the CIA, part of the money coming from opium trade. After defeating the USSR army, the same Al Qaeda turned its guns against the US, and India in particular. Their actions are equally harmful to Pakistan also, as a matter of fact currently Pakistan is the biggest victim of terror attacks from various militant groups.

Al Qaeda, Taliban have come up like a Frankenstein's monster, turning against its creators and others, like India. To understand Pakistan, we have to realise that even today, Pakistan is a divided house, civic society and elected government on one side and the

Mullahs, Al Qaeda and others along with the army and outfits like the ISI on the other. So any peace talk with Pakistan means, to make moves which strengthen the civic society and the elected government there and by pass the army and the mullahs. A blank anger against Pakistan has no place in the solution to the issue.

The Problems

The issues as seen on both sides of the border pertain to

a. The solution to the claims about Kashmir

b. The terror attacks

So far, an ad hoc pattern has been the norm in the nature of the talks and efforts between two countries. The Shimla accord, the Vajpayee bus yatra and Mushraff's Agra trip stand out as the major efforts to bring in peace. These efforts have failed to yield the desired results due to many flaws in the premises and steps taken in the direction of peace. The talk of war and efforts to resolve matters of contention has gone hand in hand. A dominant small section wants to solve the problem by war of different types, attacks on Pakistan. As pointed out, war will be a serious setback to the process of reconciliation in South Asia.

Gandhian Approach

The core of a Gandhian approach revolves around the

a. Firm and non-negotiable resolve for nonviolence as a principle.

b. Involving the masses in the process of reconciliation.

c. Process of dialogue with the 'other', based on thorough understanding of the problem.

The first point to be made in this direction is that we need to understand the plight of the Kashmiri people due to acts of terror and the heavy presence of military; their yearning for autonomy within the Indian framework too has to be kept in mind. The people of Kashmir on other side of the border have lot of social and family ties with those on this side. The whole process is also linked with the enhancement of democratic process in Pakistan, in both the Kashmirs and to undermining the role of the superpower in this region. The elected representatives of both sides need to take the dialogue to a higher level of interaction. The social arena like health, education and commerce should be opened up right away. Transport and communication has to be improved to let the people meet their families and maintain social bonds form the other side of Kashmir.

Sixty years is a long time in the region. So many changes have taken place. The geopolitical realities of the region are not what they were when India got independence and the Pakistani army, dressed as tribals invaded Kashmir and one third of Kashmir came under the control of Pakistan. Over the years, the process of democratisation has not developed much. Pakistan itself has been in the grip of military rule. Even at present, when the democratic government is ruling, the threat from non-state actors, terrorist groups originally planted by United States, are out to throttle democracy in Pakistan. The total picture of the region is very important in the solution of the problem.

Multi-pronged Approach

It is imperative that India adopts a position which leads to reduction of the hold of the United States in the region and strengthening of democratic processes in Pakistan. Only through that a process of dialogue and reconciliation can become stronger. While the healthy part of the process is that democracy is struggling to get rooted in Pakistan, it is not yet strong enough to take a radical position on Kashmir. In Indian part of Kashmir, the last two elections have been very positive and in the direction of democratisation. With this, the stage is set when the presence of military in this part of Kashmir can be reduced and civic society feels less intimidated and feels free. That will be the beginning from our side to lay the grounds of dialogue with the Kashmiris on the other side of the border.

With democracy in Pakistan and the Kashmir part of Pakistan becoming stronger, the process of awarding Visas and allowing travel between the two parts should increase as much as possible. Relatives and friends must be allowed to meet and interact and this will be a great step in the direction of a long-term solution. We can intensify the cross border trade, educational and cultural exchange for people to people bonding, a prerequisite for solution to Kashmir's problem. Some attempts are already being made in the direction, much more is necessary. The report of interlocutors discussed in the last chapter (Kashmir in Turmoil 2016), can be the major ground for path to peace.

Role of British Policies

Jaswant Singh, in his book on Jinnah, has praised Jinnah's secular nature and has held Nehru-Patel responsible for Partition of India. Many people from Pakistan praised Jaswant Singh's book sky high while here in India there was a mixed reaction. The strongest reaction came from then BJP President Rajnath Singh who hinted that any praise of Jinnah will be met with strict action. The problem with such a formulation, that Jinnah was secular and Nehru-Patel were responsible for partition, is that it is an extremely superficial analysis and does not look at the complex, multilayered phenomenon of partition. It totally bypasses the role of British rulers and the different interests of diverse classes during India's freedom movement. The response to the book is either at an emotive level, our leader versus your leader, or how dare you speak against our icon!

In the midst of the whole debate, the British snatch the cake. Historically speaking, they not only took all the measures, implemented all policies which were divisive but also accepted all the demands which led to partition. In the process they ensured that even after they left, the interests of imperial powers, the UK-USA, in the Middle East remain safe and secure. This ensured that they continue to dominate the area and retain their military and political base in the region. While the mini battle, Jinnah versus Nehru-Patel is on, the role of the major culprits of partition, the colonial powers of yesteryear and the imperialist powers of today are generally not being brought under scrutiny.

If we look at the British polices, right from the beginning there were germs of divide and rule. They saw Indian society as divided along religious lines, underplaying the fact that the real divisions were not along religious lines but along class and caste lines.

As a foundation of these polices, 'doctoring of mass consciousness' along religious lines began through specially sponsored history books. The two major ones in this direction were the six-volume '*History of India as told by her Historians*' by Elliot and Dawson and *History of India* by James Mill, who periodised Indian history into the Hindu Period, Muslim Period and British period. This periodisation gave the impression that history's period is determined by the religion of the king. Needless to say that the medieval administration of Kings was never based along religious lines; their court officials and chain of Landlords belonged to both the religions. These British sponsored accounts of history argued that Muslims rulers had enslaved India and now British have come to end the misrule of Muslim kings. Such an account became a convenient tool in the hands of Hindu communalists, Hindu Mahsabha and the RSS, to play their part of divisive politics amongst the masses. The Muslim League turned it around to say that Muslim rulers were glorious and great.

This communalisation of minds was the fertile soil on which the communalists could plant their narrow agenda of Muslim Nation and Hindu Nation. Another British historian, Sir TW Holderness, in his book *Peoples and Problems of India* mooted the idea that Hindus and Muslims regard themselves as separate nations. This book came out in 1923 and in the same year Savarkar came out with his book, *Hindutva or Who is a Hindu?,* where the same formulation was presented in a different way.

On the political chessboard, Lord Curzon, the then Viceroy of India, partitioned Bengal (1904) with communal motivation and this was probably the first concrete experiment in communalising politics on a big platform.

In partitioning India, colonialists reaped rich harvest at the cost of the people of the subcontinent, millions dead, a single entity India, divided into Pakistan, India and Bangladesh. These countries keep on spending a major part of their budgets in investing in armaments and fattening of their armed forces, something which could have been meaningfully invested for the growth and development of the region. We need to wake up from the blame game and see the real culprit.

Pakistan: Sectarian Divides

South Asia has been in the grip of sectarian violence since fairly long. During last three decades and more, particularly during the last decade, this violence has been intensifying in degree and spread. It was sad news to hear that the Christian Community of Joseph Colony, Badami Bagh Lahore, was the victim of one such violence in March 2013. In this violence, 178 houses of the low-income community, as well as shops and three churches were looted and burnt to ashes. The local Pastor was attacked and the father of Savan Masih, the youth falsely accused of blasphemy, was beaten up and subsequently arrested.

In Pakistan both non-Muslims and some Muslim sects (Shiites) have been harassed on religious grounds. As such, the major victims of such violence are the sects of Islam, Shias and Ahmadiyyas. The Ahmadiyyas have been declared as non Muslims through an act of Parliament. As such Shias, Barelvis, Sufis, Ahmadiyyas, Christians, Sikhs and Hindus are the religious minorities who have been facing the wrath of dominant communal forces in Pakistan. At the time of Partition, creation of Pakistan, the percentage of religious minorities was close to 23% and gradually it declined. The foundation of communal violence was very much there in the social thinking which regarded Pakistan as a Muslim state. Non Muslim minorities and some sects of Islam have been the victims of this violence. This violence picked up for the worse, during Zia ul Haq regime, when the Khakis and beard-cap came into a firm embrace, an alliance, which mutually boosted the power of both these groups.

In the decade of 1980s, the other factor which contributed to the rise in divisive thinking was the setting up of Madrassas, richly funded by United States for its goal of control over oil resources, for countering the Soviet occupation in Afghanistan. With these Madrassas, the US-Saudi support strengthened the Salafi, Wahabi version of Islam and this not only targeted the non-Muslims but also the Shias and Ahmadiyyas, the former being substantial in number.

This targeting of intra-Islam minorities also had some external support in the region, the Sunni factions being promoted and funded by Saudis and Shias by Iran. The Christian and Hindus were easy enough targets for these forces. In later decades, this violence at the social level came to be supplemented by the terrorist violence from sections of Al Qaeda.

The large number of Christians in Pakistan belong to the scavenger castes of undivided India. Not only are they looked down upon, most of the times the aim of violence is to dispose them of their lands. This is a very vulnerable social group. The blasphemy law has come in handy for attacking these communities. One recalls the case of Asea Bibi, who was in jail for her alleged remarks against Prophet Mohammad. She was sentenced to death. (In July 2015 the Supreme Court in Pakistan suspended the execution of the Christian woman.) Asea had fetched some water from a well, and a Muslim crowd chided her for 'polluting' the water since she was a 'dirty (low caste) Christian'. The twist of arguments led to her death sentence. Similarly in August. 2012, Rimsah Masih, a young, mentally challenged 14-year-old girl was arrested for burning the pages from the Koran.

In another instance, a Muslim mob which was coming out from the Masjid, broke into and destroyed the belongings of several Christian homes, because, as alleged by the one Muslim man who had an argument with one Christian man, the Christian had blasphemed against Islam. Quick mob justice, punish the community for the alleged work of one!

When Salmaan Taseer, the former Governor of Punjab, spoke about reformation of the blasphemy laws of Pakistan, he was killed by a member of his own security guard.

Every sectarian force develops its own tools and pretexts for attacking the minorities. The pretexts notwithstanding, the pattern are similar. In Pakistan, Muslim communal groups have been on the rise since the Zia regime. The degree of intensity of their boldness can be gauged from the fact that they openly take the credit for such violent acts. This, to some extent, shows their clout and acceptability in the system.

The trajectory of communal forces in three major countries of South Asia has been parallel but very distinctive. In India, Hindu communalism vitiated the peace and their regular targets were the non-Hindus, Christian and Muslims. In between, Sikhs were also subjected to massive violence. The increase in anti-Dalit violence during this period cannot be visibly linked with any anti-Muslim and anti-Christian violence. (In Dang, Gujarat in 1998, Tribal Christians were attacked.) Still, the study of history of this violence tells us that the intensification of anti-minority violence in early 1980s began with violence against dalits in 1981 and 1986. In Bangladesh and Pakistan, the non-Muslims are targeted and differing sects of Muslims are also subject to this violence. In Pakistan, it seems minority sects of Muslim and Christian and Hindus seem to be sailing in the same boat.

It will be interesting to note that unlike the perceptions prevailing in India, that all Muslims are anti-Hindus and supporting violence, what came to be noticed in recent anti minority violence was that the condemnation of these attacks against religious minorities by the secular groups in Pakistan. The case in point is the recent anti-Christian violence in Lahore. The people to condemn this have been the activists from Forum for Secular Pakistan, articulating the wish for a secular state in Pakistan and upholding the secular values in that country. To condemn this attack in Lahore, the Jamia community in Delhi organised a candle-light vigil and Khudai Khidmatgars issued strong statements condemning the violence against Christians in Pakistan. Many other groups have also added to the voices against such an insane act of violence.

While condemning one type of violence, the criticism dished forward is, 'why do you criticise only this communalism'? As such, the comments and criticism of democratic elements are directed against the acts which take place, irrespective of the religion of offenders and victims. The secular groups and commentators who raise their voices against violence are dubbed as being 'against this or that religion', being one sided and what not. The real issue is to be against all sort of targeting of religious minorities and intra-religious groups. We seem to be in a downward phase of history where communal elements are getting more powerful through dastardly violence against the vulnerable groups, more often, the poor of the community, but not necessarily so.

Shiv Sena Ire against Shah Rukh Khan

In January 2010, Shah Rukh Khan, the celebrated film star, voiced his opinion that Pakistani Cricket players should not be prevented from playing in IPL cricket league. This sparked a big row of protest from the local Shiv Sena supporters, who criticised Khan and tore the posters of his film, *My Name is Khan*, they also went on to say if Shah Rukh's 'Khan' is awakening, he should very well go to Pakistan and be there. At the same time Shiv Sena is spearheading a violent campaign, 'Mumbai for Maharashtrians', to which even cricket star Sachin Tendulkar, a Maharashtrian, amongst others voiced their opinion that all parts of India belong to all the Indian citizens.

Mumbai has seen turmoil around these twin issues, regionalism, and communalism, in its worst form. One knows that India-Pakistan relations have been quite strained right since the beginning. There have been three wars between these two neighbours. The people living across the borders, with relatives on either side, have been moaning with pain and anguish due to this strife between the two countries. Many issues have been a bone of contention between the two neighbours, the major being terrorism.

Terrorism needs to be understood in its depth if it is to be eliminated. The roots of this terror lie in the politics of oil and creation of Madrassas on the soil of Pakistan to train the Al Qaeda terrorists by US.

While terrorism's base might be in Pakistan, it is not the Pakistani state, or Pakistani people or democratic elements that are supporting this poisonous cancer. Not long ago, Pakistan lost its Prime Minster to terrorism and regularly we see acts of terror perpetrated in Pakistan. To eliminate this cancer, the civilian government in Pakistan is trying its own bit, but the military-mullah complex in Pakistan is the one, which nurtures this phenomenon. While we are fully justified in condemning terrorism, calling upon civilian government to control it, it is also true that gestures of friendship to Pakistan will strengthen civilian government and eliminate terrorism in the long run. So peace with Pakistan has to be strengthened through music, sports, business and educational exchange. A Hate campaign between the neighbours will be harmful to the interests of both the countries. So while anger against terrorism is natural, we can't ignore the deeper dynamics of the region and shun peace. Peace is the pre-requisite of progress of the region. The insinuations by Shiv Sena against Shah Rukh, asking him to go to Pakistan, just because his name is Muslim, is against the values of the Indian Constitution and the spirit of the National movement, which built the country. The divisive nature of regional politics is to be condemned through and through. Our concept of citizenship is not based around religion. People of all religions are equal citizens of the country. To doubt the patriotism of any citizen just because of 'one's religion' is an insult of the Indian Constitution.

In the same way, while appreciating the fact that metros like Mumbai can't accommodate the population beyond a point, there is also a need to introspect as to why so many people migrate to Mumbai? As such, it is lop-sided development of the country which forces people to migrate to such a metropolis. So while demanding a curb on Shiv Sena for its hooliganism and anti-national utterances, one also has to focus attention on a pattern of development where people don't have to migrate just to survive. That's where the crux of the matter lies and a solution to Shiv Sena's demand.

Shiv Sena has a complex history. It was supported by industrialists and partly nurtured by a section of the Congress leadership decades ago. The idea then was to smash the left trade unions, which were struggling for workers rights in an honest way. Later, the same Shiv Sena attacked the South Indians, then Gujaratis and finally North Indians for sometime before jumping on the Rath (chariot) of Hinduvta spearheaded by BJP's Lal Krishna Advani. Shiv Sena has been the most firm ally of BJP and its communal politics all through. Shiv Sena's supremo Bal Thackeray was indicted in the Srikrishna Commission report, a report which has been put into cold storage by the Congress government. Interestingly, Shiv Sena, SS, presents its role in Mumbai's violence as being that of protecting Hindus, a formulation which is from the world of make believe, which presents the victim as the culprit, as the Srikrishna Commission makes it very clear.

The methods employed by Shiv Sena earlier and MNS (Maharashtra Nav Nirnman Sena) of Raj Thackeray show the parallels with the ones employed by Hitler's foot soldiers, ie. to intimidate people through street violence. In this direction, on a regular basis, the Shiv Sena in particular attacked artistes, Gulam Ali, a Gazal singer from Pakistan, MF Husain, a great Indian painter, and now Shah Rukh Khan. In these 'storm trooper' methods the SS has been associated with the parallel forces like the RSS, the Bajrang Dal etc. The idea is to vandalise and make a glaring attack on liberal values of democracy. While outfits like the SS, MNS and Bajrang Dal are fascists, they use democratic space, and the lapses of opportunist centralist politics to come up in the social space. Hitler also used the democratic space to come, to abolish the democratic space itself. The analogies of such formations with Hitler are too glaring to be ignored. They are a product politics of vested interests, taking advantage of centrist formations like the Congress and than turning into Frankenstein's monsters.

With Bal Thackeray trying to pass on the mantle of his fascist politics, Uddhav and Raj, son and nephew respectively, claimed the inheritance. Bal Thackeray decided to anoint his son Uddhav as the heir apparent. Peeved by this, the more aggressive Raj launched his own outfit, Maharashtra Nav Nirman Sena. In the formative period of MNS, Congress again played a complicit role by sitting pretty when Raj unleashed his aggression against hapless taxi drivers from North India and Bihar. This acted as tonic for the MNS, and it became bold enough to unleash rampage time and over again. It has come to stay as a political force. The role of the Congress has been very compromising as far as formation of Shiv Sena and MNS are concerned.

Shiv Sena-MNS primarily belong to divisive-fascist anti-national ideology of communalism and regionalism. Their disregard for the values of the Indian Constitution is there for all to see. Their politics also proves that divisive ideologies strengthen each other. Both these outfits, particularly the Shiv Sena, has been using these sectarianisms for political benefit.

Shiv Sena and its offshoot, Maharashtra Nav Nirman Sena, both thrive on the divisive sentiments. The spirit of national integration is being attacked by the actions of these regional forces. We should not target our citizens in the name of religion or region. Similarly their encouragement of Hate against Pakistan is shortsighted and is playing to crude emotions, ignoring the deeper causes of terrorism. For that the finger of accusation should point to the US policies which has been pursing its politics of control in the region and has used Pakistan as the base and ally for its exploitative ambitions. One must support the rights of all our citizens within the limits of the Indian Constitution and restrain the regional and communal forces that hinder national progress.

Pakistan: Democracy Besieged

The shooting of Salman Taseer, Governor of Punajb, Pakistan (4th January 2011) by his body guard is a serious attack on liberal values in Pakistan. Taseer had opposed the blasphemy laws in Pakistan and called these laws, black laws. Salman Taseer, after his appointment as Governor of Punjab, was a vocal opponent of orthodoxy. He did have a progressive outlook and was promoter of education for girls. All this was a matter of opposition from those holding intolerant views, couched in the language of Islam. The story began with his meeting Asiya Bibi, a Christian, who had been jailed under blasphemy law. Taseer called for clemency for Bibi and also said that the minorities need to be protected in Pakistan. This annoyed the orthodox elements, and their reaction was here for all to see. In the aftermath of his death, the events in Pakistan have been a matter of grave concern. The murderer, Malki Mumtaz Hussain Kadri, has become a sort of hero for a vocal section of conservatives, while the clergy, the Mullah concerned, refused to conduct the last prayer for Taseer.

The blasphemy laws, as they exist in Pakistan, are far away from the liberal interpretation of Islam. It is widely acknowledged that the Prophet himself was totally open to criticism. Stories of his level of tolerance for dissent are poles apart from what is being propagated as 'Islamic' by the fundamentalists in Pakistan. To cap it all, even the Prime Minister of Pakistan and Chief Minister of

Punjab were noticeably silent on the Taseer killing. A year before the Taseer murder; one moderate cleric had to leave Pakistan when he received death threats for his moderate interpretation of Islam. With the murder of Taseer and the reactions observed, one is saddened with the state of affairs in Pakistan society.

The blasphemy law and other ordinances going against the grain of democratic norms and progressive values got firmly entrenched in Pakistan during the regime of Zia ul Haq, when the alliance of Military-Mullahs became stronger. As such, Pakistan society has been a victim of the opponents of democracy for a long time. Right after the formation of Pakistan, in the name of Islam, the feudal-communal elements came to the fore and increased their social and political power. With the death of Jinnah, there was no controlling factor for the communal elements and sectarian policies. As such, the very formation of Pakistan today is seen as some sort of a movement by many, while as a matter of fact, the core reason for formation of Pakistan is many a time missed out. And that core point is the long term goals-designs of colonial-imperialist powers.

England, to be soon joined by the rising power US, was determined to create a base in South Asia to counter the rising tide of Communism, socialism and nationalism, in the decade of 1940s. Imperialists perceived that these trends of national liberations were going to hamper the exploitation of nations being done by them. One can go to the extent of saying that Pakistan was deliberately created by unleashing and promoting communal forces leading to communal violence and the surrender of nationalist elements and to the rising tide of violence in the country. Leaders like Jinnah, Nehru and Patel might have their stands which seemed favourable to partition, but that is a superficial and partial layer of truth. The dynamics of 'divide and rule' did create the communal streams from the declining sections of Princes and landlords, to be joined by a section of educated middle class and elite. The national movement under Gandhi called for the secular democratic state, while the communal streams envisaged a Muslim state, a Hindu state. At surface, the argument was that this is a Hindu nation from times immemorial so we should have a Hindu state, or that Muslims will not get justice in Hindu-dominated India, so a Pakistan will be for Muslims, protecting their interests. The dynamics of politics of the feudal classes and feudal values persisted and gradually these elements and their politics transformed themselves into the modern language, retaining their core value systems vis a vis caste-gender relationships. An artificial construct of nation, based on religion, was whipped up, duly supported by the ruling colonial powers.

After partition, in Pakistan the process of social change remained much more stunted, giving rise to a situation where the prominence of Military and Mullahs under the control of the US became the major political-social power. The democratic elements in Pakistan have been struggling all through to keep alive the values of liberalism and human rights, but the odds against them have been very heavy. In Pakistan, democracy has been the victim of triple As, America, Army and Allah (Mullahs). Hanging of Zulfiqar Ali Bhutto, assassination of Benazir Bhutto and the social dominance of military has stifled the progress of democratic norms. After the coming to power of Zia ul Haq, after the formation of Al Qaeda with US support, the situation became much worse. From the decade of 1990s, the fundamentalist onslaught has affected Pakistani society in the worse direction. Pakistan has also been a victim of terrorism in a serious way.

Here, in India, while we see Pakistani society as a very homogenous one, the truth is, Pakistan has different sections and groups whose interests are very diverse. The attitude of civic leadership, for eg. the statement of Asif Ali Zardari, for amicable settlement of the Indio-Pak disputes did not gel well with the mindset of the military of that time, whose interests lays more in continuance of the strife between these two nations. The influence of Al Qaeda, and the Madrassas which came up in Pakistan to train the Al Qaeda through US support, increased the impact of fundamentalist elements and the conservative-orthodox values.

One has to conclude that it is the civic society in Pakistan that has been the major victim of US imperialism. In India, the major perception about Pakistan is that it is a place where Islam,

Muslims, and terrorism are the major residents. Amongst large sections in India, Pakistan is regarded as an enemy state. This view is again far from the total reality in Pakistan, where progressive elements are offering a strong resistance to the attacks being made by intolerant politics. Taseer's murder was, in that context, yet another attack of fundamentalism on the liberal values and democratic space in our neighbouring country. His murder was a big set back to the preservation of liberal values.

Hysterical Outpouring or Reasoned Response

How does one deal with highly provocative situations? The simplest one is to pour out one's venom and prepare or ask for revenge. This, in a way, is the short term immature response, which lands oneself in long term problems. It is easy, it sound very brave, it sounds very patriotic in the context of nations; it appeals to raw emotions and creates a mass hysteria. At another level, for the political formations, it rewards them with an increase in the size of vote banks and an improved electoral benefit. For the television anchors or print media, rousing the raw passions, sensationalising the issues, does increase the circulation or TRP ratings. The victim in both the cases is the national interest.

This was what has happened in the killing of army jawans on the Line of Actual Control (LOC) (January 2013). India believes it has been done by the Pakistan army. Pakistan flatly denies the same. Pakistan has complained to the United Nations that India has violated the cease fire around LOC and so UN should probe the matter. In contrast, India refuses the intervention of international agency on the ground that the mandate of United Nations here has lapsed four decades ago.

The components of NDA, BJP and Shiv Sena have raised their pitch. Sushma Swaraj of the BJP then stated that, 'The incident that has happened, we should take revenge... If we don't get this (Hemraj's) head, we should get ten of theirs (Pakistan army's)'. The Shiv Sena Chief, Uddahv Thackeray, and his cousin, MNS Chief Raj Thackeray have also shown their bravado in words that advise, India should break sporting ties with Pakistan and teach a lesson to Pakistan. Surely this is aimed to increase their electoral success in times to come, consolidate their vote bank. Many a TV anchor, with an eye on the TRP ratings have talked the language of revenge, increasing hysterical content and ultranationalist noises to achieve their goals.

Does this benefit Indian's national interest in the long run? The whole demand for retaliation, revenge, breaking of ties has a raw appeal to a section of society. Those who are not in power can use it to great effect for their short-sighted political, electoral goals. The TV channels and print media resorting to presentation of such tragedies in a sensational way do get away with these things. Those in power have to consider more aspects than mere electoral benefits. The same BJP, when it was leading the NDA, talked peace with the military dictator Pervez Musharraf, who was the chief architect of the Kargil war. Atal Bihari Vajpayee decades ago talked the language of ten for one, but when in power, even he had to take the bus to Lahore for a peace process.

BJP and Shiv Sena, anyway, belong to a different stable and for them any popular sentiment directed against Pakistan, in turn is directed against Indian Muslims, in turn consolidating their Hindu vote bank. BJP-Shiv Sena and supporters of its ultra nationalism have been itching for war, use of nuclear weapons against Pakistan, in a manner which shows not only their immaturity but a type of mindset which is chauvinist. In a subtle way this is an intimidation of India's Muslim minority also. In contrast though not very perfect, the Congress government had a more mature and restrained response to the brutal killings of Indian soldiers. Now let us consider what is in India's interest as far as relations with our neighbour are concerned.

The communal forces have dichotomous attitude. On the one hand they want to keep the 'hostile to the neighbour' attitude, but when in power, they try to camouflage it and take a milder stance. Pakistan-bashing has been a centre of their political propaganda all through. Issues of this type on the border have been used by a section of media in an unscrupulous way. The anti-neighbour sentiments take the better of the rational attitude about our foreign policy. At one level one recalls that in Pakistan there are sections of society, who are averse to peaceful relations between the two countries. The 26/11 2008 happened when the India Pakistan peace process was taking off. After the Mumbai massacre by Kasab and company, the equations with Pakistan came to square one. By 2013 improvement in the Visa process, Visa on arrival was being contemplated and any border violence will once again stall the healthy step about Visa and this matter will go to the freezer again.

In the wake of the 2013 LOC incident sports interactions were pushed to the backseat and Pakistani artistes who were in India were sent home as the anti-Pakistan sentiment grew. This attitude is counterproductive to the interests of both the countries. We have to realise that India-Pakistan friendship is for the good of both the countries. This peaceful Pakistan will be what will help India progress much better. The aggressive elements in both the countries are no help to improved relationship. Any talk of retaliation at this stage will further strengthen those elements who are opposed to the normalisation of relations between the two countries. Broadly, one can say that the military and military dictators in Pakistan are not much for friendship between the two countries; the democratic elements in Pakistan do desire peace in the region. After a long time the democratic regime is likely to complete its five years in power. It is such a rare phenomenon for Pakistan; the democratic process hopefully will become stronger in Pakistan and in turn help India to focus more on development issues, rather than worrying about borders in a serious way all the time.

In the moment of grief, where two soldiers were killed brutally, firm talk and restraint with the neighbour was the need of the hour. The claims of Pakistan that the killings were not done by them only meant that Pakistan's democratic regime was not in full control of affairs and that it was finding it difficult to reign in the army. The hysterical reactions on both sides only created more bad blood on both sides.

This event has been followed by many incidents of cross border terrorist attacks. '... militants, allegedly backed by the Pakistan establishment, have targeted India again and again. On Sunday, a group of militants attacked an army base in Uri. Earlier, in

January, militants launched an assault on an Indian Air Force base in Pathankot. In July 2015, even a police station in Gurdaspur was attacked.' [http://scroll.in/article/817160/the-daily-fix-modis-impractical-election-time-war-rhetoric-on-pakistan-returns-to-haunt-him-now] The latest one has been the attack in Uri (September 2016) where nearly twenty jawans of the army were killed. This has angered the whole of the country and attempts are being made to formulate a response to such attacks, which have been a regular feature of India-Pakistan relations. While hotheads may not be satisfied with anything less than an attack on Pakistan, better counsels have to prevail to see that Pakistan has many non-state actors whom Pakistan's government may not be able to control.

As such, the irritants on the border are very disturbing and destabilise the process of dialogue for peace. Most of these are centred around the issue of Kashmir. These are discussed in detail in the chapter Kashmir Turmoil 2016.

Status of Minorities

Pakistan and India got their freedom from British rule, in mid August 1947. Today, 70 years later, where do these two major countries of the subcontinent stand vis a vis their religious minorities, is the question which we need to answer to ensure a better and more democratic space.

On 11 August 2012, a mob of over 50,000, mainly Muslims, assembled in Azad Maidan to protest against the ill treatment of Muslims in Assam and Myanmar. After some speeches full of provocation and after display of some provocative posters, the mob turned violent and vented its ire against the media for not covering the plight of Assam's Muslims, displaced in the July violence involving Bodos and Muslims. Needless to say that in Assam, violence has killed more than a hundred people and over 4 lakh people, mostly Muslims and Bodos, have been displaced, right under the nose of the ruling government. Infiltrators from Pakistan burned few OB vans and also took on the police; humiliated-molested women police personnel and beat up other police personnel. While controlling the violence, the police did the firing, which lead to death of two young men. In the whole scuffle many a police personnel also got injured. Later, the Raza Academy, the organisers; issued an apology saying the meeting was infiltrated by provocateurs. However, organisers of such events cannot shun their responsibility for the whole tragedy. Any form of 'protest' has always to be on democratic lines, non-violent and the speeches in meetings have to be on moderate lines, hate speeches and inciting the mobs is not excusable under any condition.

In the same week there is news that nearly 300 Hindus have crossed over to India from Pakistan. Ostensibly, they had come into India for pilgrimage, but many of them said that they would not go back as they don't feel safe in Pakistan. Most of these Hindus are from Sind and Baluchistan. There are reports of forced abduction and conversion of Hindu girls there and the religious minorities have to live the life of second class citizens. The religious minorities persecuted in Pakistan are not just Hindus; Sikhs and Christians but also Shias and Ahmadiyyas, a sect of Islam.

Where do we find ourselves nearly six decades down the line after we committed ourselves to democracy and secular principles? India came into being as a secular democratic state and even Pakistan, which was formed in the name of Islam for the Muslim majority areas of British India, began with the secular principles as enunciated in the oft-quoted 11th August 1947 speech of Qaed-e-Azam Jinnah. In this speech, he had said that the state had nothing to do with religion; people were free to go to their mosques, temples and churches or whatever, as it was their personal matter. He also said that the white colour in Pakistan's flag represents minorities. Yet, the logic of communalism was 'built-in' in the whole system. One can make a secular speech but the social base which had resulted in formation of Pakistan, the one of feudal elements, was intact. Mere secular speeches don't change the social reality. Communalism caught up in Pakistan in due course of time and in the late seventies, with Zia ul Haq-Maulana Maududi duo ruling the roost, the mullahs came to the fore-front. The mullah-military complex backed up by the United States, which had a substantial say in the affairs of Pakistan, violated every letter and the core spirit of Mr Jinnah's speech, to the extent that today even the Muslim minorities, Shias and Ahmadiayyas are as much victims of religious intolerance and it is getting reflected in their political status in the country.

India, with Gandhi and Nehru as the major pillars of shaping the values of Indian national movement, were unshakable in their commitment to secularism. Gandhi, the devout Hindu and Nehru the atheist, had the vision of a state totally committed to respecting the people of all religious denominations, while keeping a distance from those trying to bring in matters related to faith in the ambit of the policies of state. Nehru, while doing this, realised two major handicaps. One, while our Constitution is secular, society is in the grip of religiosity so he found this as an obstacle in full implementation of secular policies. The second flaw he saw was that his party, which was founded on the grounds of secular values, was infiltrated by communal elements. There was no one to heed to his warning, and in due course, many an action of Congress leaders were indistinguishable from those of the communal elements, those forcing the country in the direction of religious nationalism.

The health of democracy in any country has to be gauged by the security and equity of minorities in the country. Through complicated mechanisms, the influence of communal elements has risen exponentially during the last three decades in particular. The whole trajectory of these two countries has been very different. While in Pakistan, there was always a space for communalism to creep in comfortably; task of communal politics became still simpler with the country falling in to the grip of Military dictatorships time and time again. The intervention of United States and US policies in Afghanistan, in particular, added fuel to the fire.

In India, the opportunism, the fallacies of the system, first past the poll, the rising anxiety of sections of society, the successful effort of communal forces to project the fear of the small minorities to the big majority and the politics around emotive issues like the building of the Ram Temple completed the picture. Today, roughly while Muslims are 13.4% in population, their percentage amongst violence victims is 90%. Today they are standing at the bottom of the socio-economic indices. The Sachar Committee has demonstrated it beyond any shadow of doubt. (The Rajinder Sachar Committee was commissioned in 2005 by Indian Prime Minister Manmohan Singh to prepare a report on the latest social, economic, and educational conditions of the Muslim community of India.) In Pakistan, the percentage of Hindu minorities has declined over a period of time and their security and social status is abominable. The injustices on minorities in one country are no justification for heaping of injustices in other country. This reactionary communalism is used by political forces in their own ways. The communal forces in India look at the Hindus being exiled from Pakistan and the Assam violence as attacks on Hindus. In Pakistan, the atrocities on Muslims in India give them a handle to further intimidate the Hindus there. In response to the Babri masjid demolition, many temples were razed to dust in Pakistan. All said and done, there is a gross contrast between the situation in Pakistan and India. Despite setbacks, the secular democratic values are the foundation of the Indian system, though very much compromised in recent decades. In Pakistan on the other hand, democracy has been of marginal value, there are efforts to root it in Pakistan but the obstacles are immense. The common factor is the suffering of minorities, though the degree of this suffering is very different in both these countries.

Where will all this lead us to? The communal issue is a big brake to the social development of the countries as a whole. The values of affirmative action for weaker sections of society, the going an extra mile to protect them and to bring them up in social area is what is needed. Seventy years after coming out from the yoke of colonialism, it is time we remember the values of Liberty, Equality and Fraternity, the principles which guided our freedom movement. In India, there is an urgent need to reform our electoral system to reflect our social and political needs. Communal violence and discrimination against minorities is an immense loss to our national ethos and humanism. Time to check it and reaffirm in practice, those values which made us India! And for Pakistan, high time to come back to the values outlined in the speech of Jinnah on 11th August 1947; decline in the percentage of minorities and their exodus from Pakistan is a great insult to the founder of Pakistan!

Can Religion be the Basis of a Nation State?

Javed Jabbar in 'The nation is made of these' (*Outlook*, 8th April 2013) appreciably makes a very strong case for defence of minority rights in Pakistan. At the same time, he makes serious omissions as far as the list of minorities is concerned. He fails to mention the Muslim sects against whom atrocities are being committed, Shia Muslims and Ahmadiyyas. The latter have been even deprived of the status of being Muslims. The reasons are obvious as Jabbar's concept of Pakistani nationalism is based on the hollow ground, that Islam is the base of Pakistani nationalism. He also gives a new twist to the formation of Bangladesh. The formation of Bangledesh irrefutably proved that religion cannot be the binding glue for a modern nation state, but he comes to change the 'two nation' theory into 'Two Nation three state theory'!

Pakistan was not a nation before its formation. In his speech, Jinnah had pointed out that a new nation was to be created in the state of Pakistan. Contrary to this, Jabbar tries to say that the process of formation of Pakistan begins with the time when first Muslims arrived in the subcontinent. This is a total distortion of the history; in a way it is falling into the trap of communal historiography, which the British introduced in this region to pursue their goal of 'divide and rule'. This linking of Muslim nationalism with the rule of Mohammad bin Kasim is parallel and opposite of the Hindu nationalists arguing that this has been a Hindu nation since times immemorial.

The very formulation that Muslims ruled for so many years or Hindus ruled from times immemorial is flawed. Mahmud Gazni had five Hindu generals in his army. Shivaji had 12 Muslim generals in his army. Akbar had Raja Mansingh as his commander in chief while Rana Pratap had Hakim Khan Sur fighting on his behalf. Thirty four per cent of court officials of Aurganzeb were Hindus, Mirza Raja Jaisingh used to come to meet Shivaji on Aurangzeb's behalf. Kingdoms are a different system of rule and to link up today's modern nationalism to the rule of kings is to fall in the trap of politics, which becomes divisive and communal in the modern times. Muslim communal historiography's claim that the British had taken over the Raj from Muslim rulers so it should be returned to Muslims is as much flawed as the formulation that we are a Hindu nation and so we should have Hindu Rashtra.

Glossing over the formation of Bangladesh as merely a failure of state structure is again an apologia for communal thinking. The very formation of Bangladesh proved that the interests even of the ruling elite of East and West Pakistan were diagonally opposite to each other. The major factor in formation of Pakistan as such begins with the reaction of feudal classes, Hindus and Muslims both, to the rising Indian nationalism. The lead founders of Muslim League and Hindu Mahasabha (the Nawab of Dhaka and the Raja of Kashi in particular) were together in United India Patriotic Association, which was formed jointly by the Muslim and Hindu landlords and kings. The role of feudal elements in trying to protect their social, economic political privileges in the garb of religion is cleverly hidden by the proponents of religious nationalism from both the sides. The British, having succeeded in their goal of splitting United India Patriotic Association into Muslim League and Hindu Mahsabha, got the best allies for lording it over the subcontinent.

While the leaders of these communal organisations, Jinnah and Savarkar, were hardly religious in their life style, the leaders of the secular democratic national movement Mahatma Gandhi and Maulana Abul Kalam Azad, both very religious, rejected the religious nationalisms and the concept of Muslim nation and Hindu nation. The Lahore resolution, which Jabbar calls the major milestone towards his brand of Islamic nationalism, was a handiwork of a small section of Muslims while the average Muslims at large opposed it. Maulana Abul Kalam Azad, who knew the history of Indian Muslims better than others, never came to support this resolution. The obvious point was that the communalist failed to see that Muslims were having different denominations in the country and that there was vast difference of history, culture, dress, food habits and language between different component units of the Indian Muslim community. This also became the ground for splitting of Pakistan in due course. And Azad could predict the trajectory of a state formed in the name of religion.

Gandhi, in his own style, pointed out that Muslims have different characteristics in different states of India and so he asked the Qaid-e- Azam that when he is talking of 'Muslims' is he talking of Muslims of Indian geography or Muslims of a Pakistan to be? One has to realise seventy years down the line that the colonialists had bigger interests in dividing India for their long term goal of confronting the rising tide of socialism. And we know how shrewdly imperialists later used Pakistan, keeping their hold on South and West Asia.

One welcomes the positive attitude of Jabbar in recommending the rights of minorities in Pakistan to live their lives with security and equity, at the same time he has to see that the very notion of Islamic identity for a nation is untenable in the current times.

The India-Pakistan Cricket Series

There was mixed response to the BCCI's decision to host the Pakistan Cricket Team in December-January for a limited-over's series (July 2012). Ex cricketers like Sunil Gavaskar and Kirti Azad were critical of this, while many others on both sides of the divide welcomed this idea. Imran Khan, ex-cricketer turned politician, welcomed the idea saying that this will pave the path for bringing normalcy to relations between the two countries through the negotiation table. For Asif Ali Zardari, the President of Pakistan, this was a step of confidence-building between the two countries.

As such, relation between these two neighbours has gone through lot of ups and downs. Despite three wars between the two countries, some of the core issues are of such a nature that they cannot be resolved through violence and war, and so these problems persist from so many decades. The South Asian countries, and India and Pakistan in particular, inherit the colonial legacy from the past and the problems related to the policy of imperialist power, the United States, at present. Issues like Kashmir, which is leading to massive suffering for Kashmiris, is a big thorn in the flesh, but it can only be resolved through a multi-layered dialogue and gradual resumption of the relationship amongst different groups. The current atmosphere of lack of trust, is a good reflection of what should not be there between good neighbours. At present, if one wants to visit Pakistan, the Visa is not easy and one is granted a city-wide Visa for Pakistan and even then, one has to report to the local police after one lands there. Many restrictions are there for those visiting from Pakistan to India.

These restrictions in the form of VISA to visit the other country keep waxing and waning. From Indian side the main influence is on the tourism in Kashmir.

The popular perception in India is that Pakistan is responsible for all acts of terror in India. While in Pakistan, many things are attributed to the role of India, its interference in Pakistan. In India, one can see that with the mention of the word Pakistan, there is an instant fright descending in the atmosphere. The attack of 26/11 is still being investigated and it has caused a lot of worsening of the image of Pakistan in the Indian psyche. As such, right since partition and more so during last three decades these images have been mutually negative. The whole politics of oil, as reflected in and around the Afghanistan-Taliban-Al Qaeda issue, has as an accomplice, the Pakistan army. The distinction between the US-Army nexus on one side and Pakistani civil society-democratic government is not much understood in India. All charges are attributed to Pakistan in general, leading to a negative feeling here. The policies of Pakistan are blamed on Indian Muslims, who in turn are supposed to be more loyal to Pakistan, an absurd and baseless assumption. This assumption was exploited in a surreal manner by the then Gujarat Chief Minister Narendra Modi. In the aftermath of the Godhra train burning-Gujarat pogrom, first he attributed the train burning to Pakistan's ISI and then kept challenging in his speeches General Parvez Musharff, the then President of Pakistan, who had usurped power from a democratic government. This went to the absurd limits of communal polarisation when, during the Gujarat elections, hoardings came up with Modi on one side and Musharraf on the other side, as if Modi was fighting election against Musharraf. The underlying message which Modi tried to give was that India is under threat from Muslims as symbolised by Musharrf and Modi is the saviour for Hindus. Musharrf was used as a symbolism for Indian Muslims. This shrewd trick helped the communal forces to consolidate themselves in Gujarat and other places, also leading to the victory of Modi in the post pogrom Gujarat elections.

As such, there is a growing realisation in both the countries that the destinies of both the countries are linked together and it is in their own interests to grow more congenial relations, which in turn will help solve most of the bilateral issues. Surely Pakistan army and the ultra nationalists-communalists in India are against such a rapprochement. Despite this, there are many elements that are longing for a peaceful south Asia. In this context, the people to people initiatives like Pak-India People's forum, which keeps linking the citizens of both the countries on many occasions, need to be strengthened. This forum also plays a positive role wherever possible like solving the issues of fishermen who are caught by the coast guards. This is one amongst many initiatives undertaken by this platform of amity and peace. Similarly, Aman ki Asha, a joint project between two big dailies, India's *Times of India* and Pakistan's *Jang* is creating ripples of peace in a slow and sustained manner.

There is a need to revive the SAARC, the joint platform of South Asian countries for regional cooperation. This platform came up with great amount of hope but seems to have lost steam from quite some time. India-Pakistan are the major players in this arena while the other South Asian countries share a lot of legacy, commonality of problems and their cooperation is in the interest of all of them. In this direction, the peace-loving individuals of South Asia have been contributing by keeping the links alive through various forums and sowing the seeds of hope. The scuttling of the planned SAARC meet in 2016 is yet another instance of how this platform is hostage to Indo-Pak relations.

Today, this longing for bilateral relations and peace is finding a growing articulation in the civil society in Pakistan as well. Pakistan army, with its own vested interests, is averse to such measures of peace, but our hope and wish has to be a stronger democracy in Pakistan, which will surely be looking forward to strengthening the bonds of amity between the two countries. It also reminds us as to how much both these countries are inflating their defence budget, year after year, projecting the threat of the 'neighbouring enemy'. This inflated defence budget is at the cost of the basic needs of social welfare, which are the dire needs in both the countries.

Surely, to begin with, both the countries not only need to restore cricket but also take steps in improving ties in the area of trade, health and education. There is also a dire need to loosen the tightness of the Visa, which is stifling bilateral visits of civilians.

Pakistan: Victim of Imperialist Designs

The tragic events of 26/11, the Mumbai terror attack, have brought forward different responses from diverse sections of society. One most common is that, since the terror groups are based in Pakistan, an attack should be launched on Pakistan to wipe out the training centers located in there. The popular yoga Guru Baba Ramdeo, with massive following, has said that this is the right time to teach a lesson to Pakistan.

Former Pakistan President, Asif Ali Zardari in an article in *New York Times*, argued that the terror training camps located in Pakistan were propped up and supported by United States to train the terrorist to fight against the Soviet occupation of Afghanistan during the cold war era. It is clear that these bases and the indoctrinated terrorists, who are a product of these camps, were brainwashed into violence on the misplace notions of Kafir, enemy, and this concept of kafir was instilled amongst the youth in these US-supported madrassas.

Will attacking Pakistan help matters? The Frankenstein's monsters created for pursuance of political goals are easy to produce and difficult to control and eradicate, once their political utility is over. Khalistanis were similarly promoted to go more and more into extremism, Sikhism was invoked as a cloak for this politics. Later, the same monster turned against the forces which aided in their creation. Not surprisingly, Al Qaeda clones later turned their guns against their creators and others.

The truth is that the US imperialism is capable of creating monsters for its political goals and then these elements continue to do the dirty tricks in times to come. The biggest harm is due to the US couching its political-economic ambitions in religious language. This has led to demonisation of a religion and a religious community, with tragic consequence for the community. So much was Islam and Muslim likened to terrorism that the average common sense stopped short of the truth of US involvement in the whole game. Our social common sense is reflected by what saffron-robed swamis say.

The state of Pakistan has been a victim of the Colonial power's design in the pre-independence era and later it has been mauled and used by USA for maintaining its hegemony in the oil rich zone. Most of the political commentators will equate formation of Pakistan as the result of Muslim separatism. The fact is that British policy of divide and rule encouraged the Muslim and Hindu elites to put up the Two Nation theory, which was initially put forward by Savarkar. Handful of elite was behind the idea of Pakistan and Hindu nation respectively, but the British gave them importance out of proportion to their social base. The politics of Hate propagated by these communal formations intensified the communal violence, resulting in severe cracks in the concept of composite Indian nationalism, leading to partition of the country. More than Muslim League it was British design of having a long term control in the region that resulted in formation of Pakistan. Hindu communalists have to share equal blame as they also said that nationalism is based on religion, that there are two nations within the country and that Muslims have to be subordinate to the Hindu nation.

US empire substituted the declining British empire and turned Pakistan into a semi vassal state, using it as its military base. In Pakistan, US hegemony is as much responsible for stifling the democratic process as the hold of the mullahs and the Army. We have to recognise that today a very positive process of rise of democracy is going on in Pakistan. The elements which will benefit by attacking Pakistan are those opposed to democracy, the mullahs and the army. US seems to have milked Pakistan as much as it needed to and is now looking for shifting its base in South Asia, and also blaming Pakistan for terror groups, forgetting its major role in the same.

Attacking Pakistan at this point is what the fanatic elements in Pakistan and India want. The response to 26/11 has been cleverly modulated into becoming anti-Pakistan hysteria. The demand for attack on Pakistan will well serve the fanatics in Pakistan and the fanatics in India both. Their interests match most of the times. It is sheer insanity to think of attacking a nuclear weapons-armed country, and it also means strengthening the arms of Pakistan army and mullahs.

The need is that of a joint endeavor by both the democratic governments to honestly investigate the Mumbai terror attacks, to punish the guilty. If possible, India should take steps which strengthen Pakistani government in its own battle against the army and mullahs. This strengthening of democratic process will help India as much as Pakistan, if not more. One can see the change in the language of Pakistan's government since the military is cooling its heels in the barracks and democratic process has taken over the centers of power. One hopes the Indian government does not fall into the trap laid by Pakistani fundamentalists and is able to overcome the exhortation-hysteria of sections calling for Pakistan's blood in the act of blind revenge, while ensuring the terror acts are controlled.

Few years down the line, now we see a gradual shift in the pro-Pakistan orientation of US policy. Earlier it was totally supporting Pakistan on every issue, with changing South Asian dynamics US stand is not so partial to Pakistan.

Death of bin Laden and a Changing World

The announcement of the death (on 2 May 2011) of Osama bin Laden is mired in many mysteries, It is also full of blatant violations of International law. It does have a profound impact on the future of global politics. Osama and Al Qaeda had been dominating the global political scenario covertly and then overtly since the last three decades. The West Asia-Indian subcontinent was a major victim of their dreaded acts; still the death of this Frankenstein's Monster has been accompanied by infinite questions and implications.

To begin with, there had been various news items claiming that Osama is dead, time and over again. Pakistan's ex Prime Minister Benazir Bhutto, who herself became a victim of the acts of terror, had said that 'Osama is already dead', several years before 2011. Anyway, what matters is the popular perceptions and the 'understanding'. This understanding 'manufactured or real', is propagated by the global emperor and the dominating US media. This seems to be more important than the truth. Truth shall ultimately prevail, but in the short run, the propaganda and perceptions do dictate the global and local scenario. So, in that sense now, Osama is really dead for good because America says so. The manner of his killing reminds us as to who is the biggest violator of international law. Here is a super power, with its tentacles spread all over the world, itching to undertake actions in the name of Democracy and Peace, but in reality, protecting its interests of controlling oil wealth and maintaining global supremacy. The US armed forces blatantly violate Pakistan's air space, ignore its sovereignty, and kill Osama. Noam Chomsky, the indefatigable Human Rights conscience keeper, poses an interesting question. What if Pakistani or some other army lands up in White House, kills someone there and dumps the body in the sea? Unthinkable, no!

Osama could have been captured and tried in the International Court of Law and punished accordingly. Why did a criminal had to be killed is beyond imagination in the civil world, with so many laws and norms. It seems laws and conventions are for ordinary mortals and states. For some states (like the US), the medieval 'Might is Right', 'We are the law', still prevail. This is a warning for the whole humanity, reminding us of the need for reviving international bodies like United Nations not just formally but de facto, with real flesh and blood. Organisations like United Nations not only need to be revived and democratised, they also have to be endowed with legal and moral authority to mediate in international affairs. The arbitrary 'cow boy' norms need to be condemned and done away with.

This 'death of Osama' should open a new chapter in global and local politics. The previous decades have been dictated by the US policy of oil hunt by creating the slogan of 'Clash of Civilizations', a slogan which is an insult to the humane values of mankind, a concept which deliberately overlooks the deeper alliance of people and civilisations. This 'clash of civilisation' thesis practiced by the US projected Islam as the threat to democracy and freedom, irrespective of the fact that it is the same global power which overthrew democracies and promoted dictatorships in the area for its economic political agenda. The overthrow of the democratically-elected Mossadeq regime in Iran (1953) had set the tone for imposition of authoritarian regimes in this area. Again, the processes which have begun in Tunisia, Egypt etc. are reminders that the Arab World Muslims aspire for democracy as much as any other people in the world and are trying to overthrow the yoke of dictatorial regimes.

The US invasions of different countries in the region were justified by projecting Islam and Muslims as backwards by the 'global super-cop', which projected the myth that it is playing the role of the saviour. With the death of Osama-bin-Laden this chapter of dark global politics should be over, and the region should be left to its own moral and political resources to develop their own political systems, away from interference by outsiders. Democracy is basically a grass roots process. It cannot be 'exported' or 'imposed' on others. The efforts should be to let the local alliances emerge, to let global democracy amongst nations emerge and let the local population decide their path for achieving the democratic system. It is on these issues that all the concerned peace movements assert the values of peace and democracy through mass demonstrations. These voices and peace campaigns should act as a brake to hegemonic policies of the superpower.

In India, terrorism was abetted by local groups; Aseemanand, Pragya Singh Thakur and others derived their pretexts from the terror acts of Osama and company. Since Hemant Karkare's landmark investigation in Malegaon blast case, series of operatives wearing saffron clothes were caught and hopefully this dreaded process will also come to an end, it will not derive provocation form other terror groups.

As far as India and Pakistan are concerned, the whole talk of repeating Abottabad by a section in India, needs to be thrown in the dustbin. The Indian political leadership has shown political maturity and offered the dialogue table for achieving friendship with this neighbour. The same should be enhanced. On one hand we firmly deal with the criminal elements, by promoting trust and amity between nations and on the other the cooperation in the area of culture, trade, commerce and education needs to be boosted. Not only restricted to Pakistan, we need to revive the spirit of SAARC at a deeper and broader level.

The assumed death of Osama has been a boon to the process of peace anyway. Later, the formation of ISIS, from the ruins of the Iraqi army and Al Qaeda ideology has kept the fire of terrorist violence going. The demonisation of Islam and Muslims will hopefully come to an end. Morality of all religions has been a great contribution to development of human values. All religious communities have contributed to the progress of the human race, and this needs to be the major slogan of coming decades.

A Nobel for Malala

Pakistan has been facing innumerable troubles, not entirely due to its own faults. The whole politics of oil, the designs of the Empire and the subservience of the mullah-military complex to US designs have brought a lot of misery in this region. The plight of young Malala Yususzai(Age 15) who had to battle for her life after she was shot twice by the Taliban (October 2012) was a well-documented incident. Her 'crime' was that she dared to defy the Taliban dictats and expressed her longing for education for herself, and for the education of other girls. When Taliban became powerful in Swat valley they shut down girls' schools and women were banned from social space till Pakistan got control over the area, but still Taliban's influence in the area did not vanish.

During this period Malala, then aged 12, started writing her diary for the BBC Urdu channel and later, a film with her at the center was made by *New York Times,* 'A Class Dismissed'. She emerged as the major voice of rebellion against fundamentalist assertiveness against education of the girl child. The Taliban, like all fundamentalist streams, uphold the oppressive patriarchal values, where social space is a strict 'no no' for women, who are supposed to take care of the kitchen, children and their life has to revolve around instructions of the Mullahs. In the transition from feudal society to democratic norms, the major change is that of caste/class and gender transformation. There is no straightforward formula for this. In the countries where the democratic revolutions were complete, the feudal norms of caste-gender hierarchy were overthrown along with the rule of Kings-feudal elements.

In former colonies, the introduction of newer set of norms of modern education, industrialisation and the consequent changes in society did bring in social movements, enabling society to come out of the grip of an older set of values. The grip of older dominating forces, kings-landlords, was not done away with totally in most post-colonial states. The newer classes, the industrialists-workers-educated classes came up side by side with the declining feudal elements. The declining sections did not disappear and so they tried to preserve and assert their values and social norms under the garb of religion, politics in the name of religion, what is popularly referred to as communalism. As such, it is abuse of religions' identity, to uphold and impose the norms of feudal society in a newer language.

In former colonies, we are particularly talking of the Indian subcontinent, the subjugated sections of society, the low caste and women had a marathon struggle to strive for equality and to come to the democratic social space. This struggle is not yet over despite seventy years of independence in the Indian part of the post partition area, while in Pakistan, the process has been slower and has seen a massive reversal after the Zia ul Haq-Maulana Maududi regime. Fundamentalism worsened with the coming up of Mujahideen-Taliban-Al Qaeda, a process supported or rather engineered by the United States and Saudi Arabia. The ideological use of Wahabi version of Islam to train Mujahedeen-Taliban interprets Islam in a backward way to enslave the women and other weaker sections of society. Pakistan society today is the victim of multiple fundamentalist phenomenons at the same time. While the US created the Taliban-Al Qaeda, today the same US-Nato wants to do away with them through drone attacks. These drone attacks are hardly a solution to the cancer which they have planted in this part of the world. Now at last, a large section of Pakistan's society is realising the anachronism and standing with the aspirations of Malala, knowing fully-well that she does represent the longing of girls of her age. Most parents in the region want their girls to be educated and wish them a future of knowledge and enlightenment. Many a scholars of Islam remind us that learning-education, both for men and women has a high place in the teachings of the Prophet, while there are many others who draw from other sources to justify the shootings of Malalas. There are peace rallies in Pakistan which are telling the fundamentalists 'Bandukon Wale Darte hain Ek Nanhi Ladki Se' (those with guns are scared of a little girl). This section well knows that their country's dilemmas stem from ideology imported from Saudi Arabia, thanks to the machinations of the CIA operating through the military-mullah complex.

The 'Malala moment' is a serious turning point for Pakistan. Which way it wants to go, which way it can make space for itself? The past cannot be changed. Today's problems created by the Taliban and its clones need a serious engagement, a 'do or die' situation for Pakistan's democracy. The persistence of Taliban is a malignant disease eating up its vitals. It needs to be put behind, this ideology and this mindset has to be thrown in the dustbin of history with total willpower, determination and efforts. Those in the subcontinent need to hold their hands for democracy and freedom. We, in the region, need to strive towards solidarity for a democratic South Asia, in order to bury the ideologies operating in the name of religion. Everyone needs to stand with the cause of Malala!

In India, the trajectory has been similar to some extent. As fundamentalism, political assertion in the garb of fundamentals of religion, rose in the West Asia-Pakistan, in India we see the rise of communalism in the name of Hindu religion with a similar agenda, which has pushed back the march of caste and gender towards equality. During 19th century, Indian women had to face something very close to what Malala and large section of girls-woman are facing today in Taliban dominated area. Savitribai Phule, who began schools for girls, had to face the wrath of the conservative sections of Indian society. As Malala has had to hide books under her shawl, a woman named Rash Sundari Devi in Bengal had to hide her longing for reading, as touching a printed paper was regarded as sin. In her autobiography Aamar Jeevan (My Life) she describes the challenges she faced as a woman who wanted to learn. She learnt reading by picking up newspapers when the men were not at home. Lot of rumors were spread to stall education of girls. The struggles of Pandita Rama bai, Anandi Gopal and many of their contemporaries, to get education, were equally harrowing. Even today girls' education is lagging behind in its reach and importance in large parts of free and democratic India.

In earlier part of the 20th Century, in the United States when social transformation for class and gender began, the conservative Christian groups opposed this social change by bringing out ten small booklets called Fundamentals, which argued against women and workers' rights in the language of religion. It is from these booklets that the term 'fundamentalism' emerged. The fundamentalist tendencies have resurfaced world over in the last three decades or so, and have been promoted by the imperialist powers. When Hitler trashed democracy in Germany in the name of 'Race', he dictated that the life of women should revolve around kitchen, church and children. Coated in sugary syrup, a similar viewpoint is being beamed through the television serials in India, where the unending 'Saas bhi Kabhi Bahu Thi…' serials dominate the small screen and give the message of subordination of women. To add to the impact of these serials, the Godmen, hordes of them who have mushroomed during the last three decades, talk of such norms in a refined language and they do have higher acceptability and sanctity. Today, in America, known for its left-liberal doctrines, we see the rise of a Donald Trump.

Nawaz Sharif's Visit to India

India-Pakistan relations have always been mired in various controversies, which have been preventing friendly relations between the neighbours, who in 'popular perception' are respectively seen as an enemy. It is due to this that while all the members of SAARC countries have been invited, the one to draw maximum popular attention was the coming of Pakistan President Nawaz Sharif, the president of Pakistan to Prime Minister Narendra Modi's swearing-in ceremony. In a deft move, India's Prime Minister had sent an invite to all the heads of SAARC countries for the event (16 May 2014), which was held with great pomp and show.

Nawaz Sharif faced lots of obstacles in accepting this invitation. His family, his daughter included, tweeted and called for acceptance of the invite, she wanted to know why India and Pakistan are living in a hostile situation like North and South Korea, why can't they live like the countries of the European Union? She was actually echoing the sentiments of most Pakistanis who want the strengthening of democracy in Pakistan and good relations with India; she articulated the aspirations of Pakistan's majority for whom peace with India is synonymous with the path of good democracy and development. In my own visit to Pakistan a couple of years ago, I was overwhelmed with expressions of longing for friendship with India. This also gets reflected in their warm gestures in welcoming you, and showering the best of hospitality on you. Major obstacles in Pakistan to peace with India come from the strong army and the mullah alliance. In 2014, even as the Modi invite was in the pipe line, a terrorist attack took place on the Indian Consulate in Afghanistan, in Herat. The Hafiz Sayeeds of Pakistan raised their eyebrows and dished out the usual threats. One also recalls that the horrific terrorist attack on Mumbai on 26/11 2008 took place when the process of peace between India and Pakistan was to pick up. The correlation between the steps of Indo-Pak peace process and attacks of terror, in which the hand of terrorist groups has been identified, have their support from the some army quarters, is unmistakable.

During the previous NDA regime, when Atal Bihari Vajpayee wanted to initiate peace with Pakistan and took the friendship bus to Lahore, the then Pakistan army did not welcome it and expressed its reaction by occupying Kargil. Pervez Musharraf was the army Chief then. This Kargil occupation by Pakistan army had to be fought by Indian army, supported by President Clinton urging Pakistan to withdraw from Kargil. During my Pakistan trip, I also happened to meet the activists who are committed to friendship with India. These activists, along with their counter parts in India, have been promoting forums like the Pak-India People's Forum. They are also promoting peace and are campaigning for the release of innocent fishermen who get arrested here and there. Nawaz Sharif releasing the fishermen before his visit to India was a positive gesture towards better relations with India and, in turn, a peaceful South Asia. I also had a chance meeting with those working for and identifying with the work of 'Aman Ki Asha', a joint platform of a major Indian daily along with a Pakistan daily. Here in India, the major rhetoric against Pakistan is mainly by the BJP, when it is not in power. The BJP has a contradictory attitude vis-a-vis Pakistan. When not in power; the BJP has been using Pakistan-bashing to polarise the Indian society along religious lines. When in power, it offers an olive branch and releases pigeons of peace. One recalls that our present Prime Minister had brought polarisation in Gujarat after the Godhra tragedy and Gujarat carnage by primarily attacking Pakistan and its President, Pervez Musharraf. Even during the election campaign of 2014, Modi did resort to menacing gestures towards Pakistan. His party colleague Giriraj Singh was very abusive to Pakistan. The 'social-communal common sense' is so constructed as if the Indian Muslim is loyal to Pakistan. The Indo-Pak cricket matches are seen more as India-Pakistan war rather than a sport which should act as a bridge between the countries in a sportsman's spirit. Irrespective of the fact that it was Madhu Gupta who was caught spying for Pakistan, the major feeling is to suspect every Muslim as a potential Pakistan spy. Our legendary film star Dilip Kumar (Yusuf Khan) was humiliated time and time again for his accepting Pakistan's highest civilian award, Nishan-e-Pakistan. Rumors against Dilip Kumar were circulating on regular basis. Every skirmish on the border is used to denigrate Pakistan and at the same time, criticise Congress for its 'soft' approach to the issues. The anti-Pakistan rhetoric is one of the major tools in the hands of BJP, when it is not in power.

Its ally, the Shiv Sena, goes one step forward. It has regularly created ruckus on every occasion of Pakistan-India interaction. It dug up the pitch on a cricket ground to prevent a match, programmes of Pakistan artists are disrupted and even in 2014, when Nawaz Sharif decided to come, Shiv Sena threatened to boycott the PM's oath-taking ceremony. Fortunately, wiser counsels prevailed.

Unfortunately today, in whole of South Asia, religious minorities are going through rough weather, Christians and Hindus in Pakistan, Hindus and Muslims in India, Hindus and Buddhists in Bangladesh and Hindus in Sri Lanka. The violation of the rights of minorities needs to be halted through mutual talks and cooperation. The atrocities on minorities in one country cannot be undone by atrocities on the other ones in another country. Every innocent person, irrespective of her faith, has a full right to follow one's faith. This can be a major agenda for reconciliation in SAARC in the times to come.

As far as Pakistan is concerned, more the democracy becomes strong there, the hold of the army weakens and the peace process will become stronger. The strength of the stranglehold of the army in Pakistan is inversely proportional to the health of the democracy and friendship with India. While in India, the democratic ground is stronger, a positive attitude to the democratic government of Pakistan will empower it vis-a-vis the feudal-army-mullah forces there, in turn strengthening the peace and making us focus more on basic needs of the people related to health, nutrition, education, employment rather than increasing the defense budget. It will help us to focus more on bread and butter rather than on guns and ammunition.

With the Uri attack (2016) by the terrorists, the equations are fast changing and it will take a while before the peace process is brought back on the wheels. After this attack, not only has the SAARC meet 2016 been cancelled, Pakistani actors and singers working in India and very popular, have been forced to leave India. Showing of Indian films in Pakistan has also been stopped, Pakistan's MNF status vis-à-vis India is being reconsidered and export of fruits and vegetable to Pakistan are also being halted. So much for India's soft power in the region.

Where Imperialists and Communalists meet!

Kashmir has been bleeding regularly. The green valley has deep patches of red. The red stains of the blood of innocent Kashmiris, the militants and the armed forces. There is hardly a week when one does not read of the killings of Kashmiris, killings by militants of this or the other hue. In the crossfire between the army and militants, many a lay Kashmiri citizen meets his doom. While Pakistan claims that by the logic of the 'Two Nation' theory, Kashmir belongs to Pakistan, India asserts that by the virtue of the treaty of accession Kashmir is an integral part of India. When one of these countries wants to talk, the other backs out and in this game of hide and seek between the two nations, the real victims are Kashmiri people and the ethos of Kashmiriyat, which are the distinctive and proud heritage of that land. Many thinkers and political forces have been contributing 'solutions' to the problem. Barring the opinion of Kashmiris, all other solutions regularly do the sympathetic rounds in the corridors of powers and in the minds of dominant social sections.

It is in this light that the recent 'considered prescriptions' of first the VHP, and then the Sangh parivar Patriarch, the RSS, are to be seen. VHP has demanded that Jammu be made a separate State, Ladhak be made a Union territory and a separate union territory be carved out from the valley for the Kashmiri Pandits. RSS has endorsed the first three prescriptions and these are similar to what the BJP had been demanding when not in power. One wants to examine as to how this solution is close to the one being proffered by US think tanks. Way back in 1953, RL Stevenson had advised Sheikh Abdullah on similar lines. In a way it is the 'best endorsement' of the Jinnah-Savarkar two-nation theory. As per this theory, the religious community determines the nationality and religion is the base of the Nation state. The only difference between these two worthies was that one said that since it is a Hindu Nation, the 'others' have to accept the primacy of Hindus and live accordingly (Savarkar). Jinnah, claiming that once the British leave, the Hindus, since they are in majority, will dominate the Muslims. He wanted Pakistan for only Muslims.

His argument was, by the same Hindu logic, as Muslims are a separate nation, so they should have a separate state.

Even at that time the British colonial powers had accepted Muslim League as the representative of Muslims and regarded Congress as a Hindu body (many a Hindu communalists were part of Congress then, but predominantly it represented all communities of India) and so the representative of Hindus. The very understanding of the British was based on the concept that India is a conglomeration of Religious communities, mainly Hindus and Muslims. The Indian national movement had to grow against the powers of the British empire and against the communal outfits of the Muslim League (Islamic state), the Hindu Mahasabha and the RSS (Hindu Rashtra). The electoral arena proved without doubt that Muslim League was no representative of Muslims, neither was Hindu Mahasabha representative of Hindus. The British at their home were seeing themselves primarily as British, but in the subcontinent they used exclusively religious categories to understand and describe India. Accordingly, when JS Mill wrote a history primer for the training of British officers, he described the periods of Indian history as Hindu, Muslim and British period. The latter was not to be described and understood as Christian period of Indian history. The Indian nation, howsoever imperfect, was in the process of formation. Different communities were bringing forth their Indian identity as the foremost identity, while relegating the religious and regional identities to the secondary positions.

The communalists and British colonialists had the same wavelength in their understanding. British also had the interest of maintaining control over their empire with a the divide and rule policy, for which, Jinnah's Muslim League on one side and the Hindu Mahasabha-RSS on the other came in handy. The colonialists and the communalists had a cozy relationship at a deeper ideological level. Communalists did not have to struggle against the British. British did not have to restrain them except when they exceeded their limits in hating each other. Unfortunately, this 'perfect ideological fit' of communalists and colonialists resulted in the Partition tragedy.

Bibliography

Amitabh Matto, 'Divide and Rue', *Times of India*, Oct.6, 2000.

Asghar Ali Engineer, 'Can Autonomy be the solution', *One India One People*, September, 2000.

Balraj Puri, *Kashmir.* Orient Longman, Tract for the Times series 4, 1993.

Balaraj Puri, 'De-alienating Kashmiris', *One India One People*, September, 2000.

GMD Sufi, *Kashmir* Vol I, 1974.

Jawaharlal Nehru Selected Works, Second Series; vol.18; p.421.

Lord Mountbatten, 'White Paper on Jammu and Kashmir', Government of India, New Delhi 1948.

Praful Bidwai, move on Kashmir, *Rediff.com*, 29 April 2003.

Press Council Committee Report, 'Crisis and Credibility', New Delhi June 1991.

Puniyani Ram, *Communal Politics: Facts versus Myths*, Sage Delhi 2003.

SK Kulkarni, 'The History of Accession', *One India One People*, September, 2000, P 9.

THE KASHMIR IMBROGLIO

For a Peaceful Solution of the Kashmir Question

The world is witnessing a series of acts of violence, political violence, which are being called 'terrorism'. The term, while difficult to define, stands for the phenomenon which uses violence for its political goals and in the process many innocents loose their lives. There are deeper causes of terrorism prevalent all over the world. The perception about terrorism also changes according to whose viewpoint one is looking at—from those committing it and those sympathetic to the cause, to the other observers, victims and their families, and the political powers. Some of these are seen as freedom movements, movements for azadi or nationhood by the participant groups, while the global powers and state apparatus are out to hunt them as terrorists.

While people from different religions happen to participate, indulge in these acts, since the last one decade the myth has been popularised that they are done by Muslims because of the teachings of Islam. While formulating this, it is undermined and hidden that people of LTTE and ULFA are predominantly Hindus, the Khalistanis, till few years ago were Sikhs, the Irish Republican Army is constituted of Chatholic Christians and there are Buddhist monks who have indulged in it in Sri Lanka and a Jew bomber had also dropped a bomb on a hotel in Cairo.

Somehow, in the popular psyche, the impression has sunk deep, that it is only Muslims who indulge in terrorism and then it is linked to Islam. The deeper processes of causes of terrorism are ignored and a superficial biased view is presented. This has been manufactured and propagated by the US state machinery, its propaganda machinery globally. The principle, which the US is propagating, is the one related to 'Clash of Civilizations'. This formulation states that the major conflict in today's world pertains to the clash between the advanced Western civilisations being attacked by the backward Islamic civilisation.

At home in India, the same type of concoctions are being put forward and the RSS combine's communal propaganda, which has been presenting a distorted version of history of the medieval times, partition tragedy and Kashmir issue, also propagates that the Muslims are the ones who are terrorists. Adding on to other issues, Kashmir has also been cited as one of the demonstrating factors, showing that Muslims are trouble-makers, are separatists and so the Kashmir problem. The Kashmir issue has been one of the legacies of the partition process and the formation of Pakistan on the basis of Islam, partly endorsing the Two Nation Theory propounded by the communalists.

Kashmir is being presented as a Hindu-Muslim problem, problem arising due to the separatism of Muslims, which it is not. The complex political factors starting from the imperialist designs of having a foothold in the region through Pakistan, and the suppression of the aspirations of the Kashmiri people have created the problem, which tends to be undermined.

The Backdrop

We will try to see the genesis of the Kashmir issue and try to understand how militancy has come to be in Kashmir. Is it due to teachings of Islam, nature of Muslims or the deeper political processes, which have resulted in this horrific situation for the people of Kashmir? As such, Kashmiri militants have been dime a dozen, each with a separate mandate and agenda. In the whole process, the Kashmiri people are the biggest victims of militancy and the average civilian is as much a victim of the dastardly acts of the militants as of the atrocities perpetrated by the Indian military, which is seen as an 'occupation army' by the native

Kashmiris. The major source of revenue for Kashmiri people, tourism, is under cloud and the local population is suffering not only political trauma but is also facing economic hardships.

Communal groups have used this to spread hatred between the two major communities. The image has been created of Muslim separatism, Islam's fanaticism etc with great intensity. While the real problems, those pertaining to wishes, aspirations and development of Kashmiri people, have been put under the carpet, the 'Hate politics' built around myths of the 'Kashmiri problem' is growing. The two diametrically opposite positions are face-to-face and irreconcilable. India has been claiming Kashmir to be its integral part and Pakistan has been putting out similar claims. Sandwiched between these opposite viewpoints, the Kashmiri people are caught in the crossfire of unending violence.

We must look at the problem from the beginning, as there are many unsolved issues associated with the tragedy of Partition and accession of Kashmir to India.

Kashmir was one of the princely States, not ruled by the British directly. The trajectory of events leading to Kashmir can be traced to the rise of Muslim communal politics in the form of the Muslim League and Hindu communal politics around the Hindu Mahasabha and the RSS. The British rulers took advantage of these feudal elements and implemented their policy of divide and rule to the hilt. Dogra dynasty's King Hari Singh, who refused to join the Constituent Assembly under the Cabinet Mission Plan ruled Kashmir. Eighty per cent population of Kashmir was Muslim while its ruler was Hindu. The Maharaja had two options, one to remain independent, two either to merge with India or with Pakistan. History says, the Maharaja wanted to remain independent. The Hindu leaders of Jammu supported the Maharaja. The J&K Rajya Hindu Sabha, including the factions who later on joined the Bharatiya Jana Sangh, the predecessor of the present-day BJP, also took this line. 'He was supported by loyal Hindu leaders from Jammu who vociferously argued that a "Hindu" State, as Jammu and Kashmir claimed to be, should not merge its identity with secular India (Puri, 1993, 5).' They were later to change their stance and wanted the Maharaja to decide in favor of accession to India.

The All Jammu and Kashmir Muslim Conference also wanted Kashmir to remain independent, with a new constitution. Interestingly, those who like Balraj Puri, a seasoned journalist of repute from Kashmir, raised the pro-India voices were dubbed as 'anti-Hindu' traitors. Congress was urging all the States to merge with one or the other dominion, which were going to result due to the partition. Lord Mountbatten also took the same position, urging all the princely States to merge with one or the other dominion, while Jinnah said that these princely States could remain independent if they so wished.

Maharaja Hari Singh was fearful of his rights being taken away due to Kashmir's merger with India and so preferred to remain 'independent' and said that he wants to make Kashmir the Switzerland of the East. He opined that the population of the State depends on tourist revenue, so it is the best course for the people of Kashmir that Kashmir remains 'independent' so that people from all the countries can come for tourism with ease. He offered standstill agreements to both India and Pakistan. India refused this offer while Pakistan accepted it. Under the terms of division of the country, central departments of State coming under the Lahore circle were all to come under the jurisdiction of Pakistan. 'Accordingly, Pakistani flags fluttered all over the offices of the post and telegraph department all over the State. (Puri, 19936)' India insisted on prior negotiations and so no agreement could be reached.

Aftermath of Partition

In October 1947, there started communal riots, as aftermath of Partition of India and the J&K State machinery was ill-equipped to handle the riots. At the same time, the Maharaja appointed Bakshi Tekchand to formulate the Constitution of Jammu &Kashmir. But around this time, Pathan tribal invaders were let loose by Pakistan to march to Srinagar. The Maharaja flew away from Srinagar for personal safety, leaving the security of Kashmir to the National Conference (party) and its leader, Sheikh Abdullah. The invaders were not welcome as Kashmiri psyche was far away from being communal. There were deep-set values of kashmiriyat, which refused to give primacy to religion as the determining factor for political behavior. This is where lay the peculiarity of Kashmir. 'Kashmir has been a melting pot of ideas and cultures. It received every new creed with discrimination and enriched it with its own contribution, without throwing away its earlier acquisitions (Puri, 1993, 9).'

GMD Sufi, in his monumental work on Kashmir, says, 'the cult of Buddha, the teachings of Vedanta, the mysticism of Islam have one after another found a congenial home in Kashmir (Sufi, 1974, 19)'. Due to this integration, people coming from all the distant lands got mixed with Kashmiri Muslims in culture, civilisation and through matrimonial relations so that all non-Kashmiri traces were totally subdued in their lives. Alien rules in Kashmir, from the annexation of Kashmir by Emperor Akbar, and through various other lineages, ultimately descended to the Dogra rulers, King Hari Singh being a non-Kashmiri, non-Muslim ruler. Parallel to the struggle of the Indian National Congress, the National Conference, a local Kashmiri party, began its movement against the king, which culminated in the Quit Kashmir movement.

Accession Treaty

Contrary to Jinnah's stand that sovereignty belongs to the Maharaja, Gandhi and Nehru held that sovereignty belongs to the people. Jinnah's opinion and Pakistan's actions were polar contrast to the secular democratic opinions of Gandhi and Nehru and no wonder that the latter, along with the Indian state principles, were more in tune with the thinking of Kashmiri people and their leadership in the form of National Conference and Sheikh Abdullah. The Maharaja, under pressure and due to his inability to protect Kashmir, requested the Indian government to bail him out of this problem. The Indian government wanted the State to accede to India before it could send in armed forces to ward off aggressors from Pakistan. The accession treaty was signed with the provision of article 370. It was not a merger. India was to look after defense, currency, foreign affairs and communication while Kashmir was to have its own constitution, flag, Sadar-i-Riyasat and Prime Minister. Justifying India's action, Pandit

Nehru in a broadcast to the Nation on 2 November 1947, said, '...Both, the Kashmir government and the National Conference, pressed us to accept this accession and to send troops by air, but made condition that the accession would have to be considered by the people of Kashmir later, when peace and order were established...(Nehru, CW, XVIII, 421)'. India approached the UN with a request to get the aggression vacated and to supervise in the process of plebiscite. The process and the linkage of vacation of aggression and the plebiscite did create a problem in due course, and eventually, holding of plebiscite got postponed sine die.

Subcultures

Kashmir is multi-ethnic. It has five regions. Though there was good deal of intermingling, there was also some specificity of each area. There were the vast northern areas of Gilgit and Baltistan, which are now directly administered by Islamabad; then there was the predominantly Punjabi Muslim strip on the western side which we now call PoK; the huge, sprawling Buddhist region of Laddakh with its Tibetan and Central Asian cultural influences is still with India; the plains of Jammu region and, finally the Kashmir Valley, with its unique cultural and historical heritage. Like it or not, two of these five regions have been under Pakistani control for over half a century.

The accession was to be subject to the ratification of the wishes of the Kashmiri people. The issue was referred to the United Nations Security Council for a peaceful settlement. Lord Mountbatten, then Governor General of India, wrote, 'Consistent with their policy where the issue of accession is under dispute, the question of accession should be decided in accordance with the wishes of people of the state. It is my government's wish that, as soon as law and order have been restored in Kashmir and its soil cleared of invaders, the question of state should be settled by a reference to the people (Mountbatten, 1948).'

An emergency government under Sheikh Abdullah took over in Kashmir. UN was approached for resolving the issue, which passed a resolution for plebiscite in Kashmir, which could not take place due to intransigence of Pakistan in not vacating the aggression. In 1951, elections were held in Indian part of Kashmir and National Conference came to power as the peoples' choice. As pointed out in the accession treaty, J&K was granted a special status under Article 370 of the Constitution. Another point to be noted here is that in the1952 talks between Nehru and Sheikh Abdullah, there was a proposal to grant regional autonomies to different areas within Kashmir, but this was never implemented. By now Praja Parishad, a close ally of the Jana Sangh, the predecessor of BJP, pressed for total merger of Kashmir to India.

Alienation of Kashmiris

Major factor in the process of alienation of Kashmir from India began with Jana Sangh Chief Shyama Prasad Mookerjee's insistence, supported openly by the Jana Sangh and covertly by some bigwigs in the Congress as well, for the total merger of Kashmir with India. At this point, Nehru was under outside pressure of Jana Sangh and internal pressure from some of his colleagues in the cabinet to totally integrate Kashmir with India. Nehru, in his wisdom could say, 'We have to be men of vision and there has to be a broad-minded acceptance of facts in order to integrate really. And real integration comes from the mind and the heart and not of some clause, which you may impose, on other people.'

Nehru, despite his own beliefs, could not hold on to a policy of trust in the popular Kashmiri leadership and the same mistake was to be repeated by successive Prime Ministers, resulting in intensification of alienation of Kashmiri people over a period of time. Asghar Ali Engineer (2000, 17) sums up the beginning of the process of alienation of Kashmir very well, '... the original sin was committed by the Congress government during the Prime Minister-ship of Pandit Jawaharlal Nehru. Nehru was emotionally attached to Kashmir and it is difficult to say whether he was genuinely disposed towards letting Kashmir have autonomy, as laid down under the article 370. After the arrest of Sheikh Abdullah... the center was more than anxious to water down Kashmir's autonomy and wanted to retain the state's grip on Kashmir. With pliable Chief Ministers succeeding the Sheikh, it was not difficult. The Kashmir Assembly passed resolutions to slowly surrender its autonomy. First, it abolished the posts of Sadr-e-Riyasat and Prime Minister and replaced them with Governor and Chief Minister, and then asked for jurisdiction of the Supreme Court to be extended to the state. By the time Sheikh Abdullah was released, all these autonomy measures were surrendered by state assembly voluntarily…'

After the death of Shyama Prasad Mookerjee, these elements became more assertive in changing the State-Center relations in the direction of suppression of autonomy granted to Kashmir, as per the treaty of accession. Sheikh Abdullah, who was so far hailed as a patriot, started being dubbed as traitor and a Muslim communalist. Sheikh Abdullah, who had so far felt that threat to Kashmiri identity came from Pakistan, now started feeling the threat of suppression of Kashmiriyat from India. 'Giving vent to popular sentiments, he started equivocating on the issue of accession. Some more factors aggravated the situation which eventually led to his dismissal from power and detention on August 9, 1953. The year 1953 thus symbolised the emotional rupture of Kashmir from rest of India. (Puri, 2000, 11)' This accusation on Abdullah, who was champion of accession of Kashmir to India, was in due course to become the seed, which later grew into the tree of alienation.

The post-Nehru era was to worsen this alienation by extending more provisions of the Indian Constitution to Kashmir. This was to provoke big hostility and anger amongst Kashmiri nationalists. 'The wave of anger provoked by fresh threats to identity of Kashmir tempted Pakistan to send thousands of armed infiltrators to the State. They got no response from the Kashmiri people as, though anti-India, they did not prefer Pak "Liberators" (Puri, 2000, 11).'

The 1971 war and break up of Pakistan led to fresh dialogue between Abdullah and Indian leaders. Abdullah returned to power after his demand for restoration of pre-1953 status of the State was conceded while he, in turn, conceded the right to the region's autonomy. In one of the fairest elections ever to be held in Kashmir, the Sheikh proved his popularity on the electoral arena when he literally swept the polls. In the elections in 1983, the Sheikh's son who inherited the mantle of leadership of the National Conference won the elections but Rajiv Gandhi illegally dismissed his government and he could become the Chief Minister only in 1986 when he agreed to share power with the Congress, leaving a void in the Opposition. This void in the Opposition was gradually filled by the Muslim United Front, which tried to capitalise on the feelings of deep humiliation caused by Farooq's coalition with the Congress, which had dismissed it in a humiliating way. 'They manipulated elections of 1987, blocked the democratic and secular outlet of discontent. In sheer desperation, a group of young men, including some candidates whose elections were maneuvered, and their polling agents took to the gun. (Puri, 2000, 11)'

This gave a good opportunity to Pakistan to use the question of Kashmir's liberation as the cause, for which, it systematically started training volunteers under the aegis of Jammu and Kashmir Liberation Front. Taking advantage of local alienation of people from the Indian state, Pakistan gradually intensified the training of militants. The Pakistani government, having realised the anti-India sentiments of Kashmir people, turned the 'Independent Kashmir' option into a pro-Pakistan option. This caused disillusionment amongst local people, so Pakistan started recruiting more and more external militants who were ruthless in death and destruction of property and lives, both of Hindus as well Muslims.

Militancy

The militants, most of whom were trained and recruited from neighboring countries, especially Pakistan did maximum damage to communal amity. So far, the local militants could never think of a Hindu Muslim divide, as both these communities stood together, as Kashmiris. It is worth noting that in the 1996 elections to the state assembly, the National Conference contested the elections on the basis of autonomy within India and autonomy of regions within the State, and it won all the seats barring one. Farooq kept shifting his loyalties to the party in power in the center, giving the message that Kashmir does not have the option of opposing the ruling government at the center, confirming its status as a colony of the Center.

There have been repeated dismissals of the democratically-elected governments in Kashmir in order to extend the laws from the Indian Constitution in Kashmir and every such attempt has widened the gulf between India and the people of Kashmir. There have been five major attempts to restrict the autonomy of the State and yet maintain peace.

a. 1952-Agreement between Sheikh Abdullah and Nehru, the Indian government agrees to provide autonomy within India.

b. 1974-Agreement between G Parthsarthy (Indira Gandhi's emissary) and Afzal Beg affirms right of Jammu and Kashmir to have its own laws on matters mentioned in the State Constitution.

c. 1995-Narsimha Rao declares that short of azadi, 'sky is the limit' for Kashmir, but within the Indian Constitution.

d. July 2000-Deve Gowda promises 'maximum autonomy' to J&K, as it is a special State needing special treatment (Outlook, 10 July 2000).

e. July 2001-The Agra summit calling for peace is thwarted by hard core RSS combine, through Lal Krishna Advani.

Chronology of Struggle:

1. Peaceful protests crushed-1987-89
2. Armed militancy began-1989
3. Exodus of youth to PoK- March 1990 onwards
4. Decimation of JKLF -1992
5. Emergence of Hijbul Mujahideen- 1992-93
6. Entry of Foreign militants-1995
7. Restoration of 'part' democracy in 2002 elections

Democratic Ethos

In Jammu and Kashmir, the democratically elected governments have been suspended innumerable number of times. Practically all the Chief Ministers have met this fate at least once, and in some cases more than once. This, in a way, indicates the attitude of the Central government towards the democratic process in J&K.

The major blow to the sentiments of Kashmiri people came in

1984 when Governor Jagamohan sacked the duly-elected Farooq Abdullah government. It gave a clear signal to people of the State that there is no question of Kashmir's right to secede from India, it can not even have its own democratically-elected government in power. It took the level of alienation to a higher and probably irreversible pitch. This gradual destruction of Kashmiri identity, coupled with alienation, forced the people of Kashmir to fall into the lap of Muslim identity. And discontent in the valley could easily be given anti-India turn by the vested elements.

Right from the beginning, people of Kashmir had more sympathies with India due to its secular leadership. Pakistan, an overtly Muslim state, was very unpopular in the psyche of Kashmir due to various reasons. Firstly, in Kashmir itself, the movement of National Conference led by Sheikh Abdullah was founded on secular principles and he had some following in Jammu and more of it in the Kashmir valley. India's anxiety to integrate the State in the Indian union, overruling the democratic process resulted in the gradual alienation of the people.

Suppression of Kashmiri identity resulted in the emergence of Muslim identity in due course. Despite the emergence of Muslim identity, the strength of the Kashmiri identity ensured a total absence of the inter-communal strife amongst its people, marked by total absence of communal riots. Pakistan's attempt to encash on the alienation of Kashmiri people did result in targeting of Hindus and Muslims in a differential way but the place of Hindus in Kashmiri people's psyche is etched in the language and culture of Kashmiriyat, which even the nefarious designs of Pakistan-inspired militancy, could not erase. Pandit Nehru made it abundantly clear when he said in the Constituent Assembly in 5 March 1948 that, '...We would not have gone there (Kashmir) in spite of the invitation of the Maharaja of Kashmir, if that invitation had not been backed by the representations of Kashmir... (Nehru, vol.XVIII, 421).' Despite the lucrative offer of powers to the Maharaja and the predominant Muslim population which was free to go to Pakistan, they did not do so mainly because of their aspirations for secular syncretic values which they wanted to preserve.

Kashmiriyat or Hindu, Muslim Issue?

The issues in Kashmir started looking like Hindu-Muslim problems mainly because of suppression of democratic freedom, violation of the Accession Treaty and erosion of Kashmiriyat, the Kashmiri ethnic identity, and the identity which filled this gap was that of Islam. This was the golden opportunity for the nefarious designs of the Pakistani military-mullah regime to give a communal colour to the whole issue, to which the role of mistrust of the popular leadership played an ideal foil.

People of Kashmir had enough opportunity to opt for merger with Pakistan. As Jinnah was promising more powers to the Maharaja and also to accepting his sovereignty, the Maharaja also tilted towards Pakistan for a while. As I pointed out earlier, Pakistani flags were also hoisted on the buildings of the Post and Telegraph departments. But Kashmiri people, the Muslim majority, never wanted to be a part of Pakistan. It spurned the idea including the military aggression and opposed Kashmir's merger with Pakistan. Despite the severe alienation resulting due to the policies of India's rulers, due to suppression of their ethnic aspirations, due to repeated dismissal of popular governments by the Indian government, Kashmiri people even today are not opting for Pakistan as the alternative. Their main demand has been to preserve their autonomy as promised in the treaty of accession; their main aspiration is to preserve the ethnic character of Kashmir and to be able to live life away from the crossfire resulting from the interference of Pakistan and mistrust of the Indian state.

An opinion polls conducted by *Outlook* (16 October 2000) reveals that according to 74% of the respondents, separate identity of Kashmir is what is required, 16% favored greater autonomy and only 2% wanted merger with Pakistan. As many as 39% felt that a solution could be found within the framework of the Indian Constitution.

The major spurt in militant activities took place from 1990 onwards. We will have a look at some of the figures of the casualties and destruction of property in Kashmir by militants from abroad:

Killings in militancy-related violence in Jammu and Kashmir

(Based on Research of Strategic Foresight Group, Courtesy Communalism Combat Jan 2005, Page 14)

Year	Hindu	Muslim	Sikh	Others	Total
1988	0	29	0	0	**29**
1989	6	73	0	0	**79**
1990	177	679	6	6	**868**
1991	34	549	6	11	**600**
1992	67	747	10	45	**869**
1993	88	891	4	44	**1027**
1994	104	835	11	73	**1023**
1995	97	1013	4	51	**1165**
1996	114	1175	2	44	**1335**
1997	64	717	1	59	**841**
1998	159	678	1	40	**878**
1999	98	648	0	17	**763**
2000	132	661	40	9	**842**
Total	**1140**	**8695**	**85**	**399**	**10319**
Percent	**11.0%**	**84.3%**	**0.8%**	**3.9%**	**100%**

Before we come to the complex problem of Kashmiri Pandits, let's understand that thousands of Muslims from different parts of the Kashmir valley have migrated to the neighbouring Himachal Pradesh in search of employment. Over 40,000 also live in a refugee camp in New Delhi. They have also taken to various jobs like coolies etc in neighbouring States. One of the *Times of India* reports (5th February1992) based on official figures said that militants killed 1,585 men and women, including 982 Muslims, 218 Hindus, 23 Sikhs and 363 security personnel between January 1990 and October 1992.

Kashmir at Crossroads

Since the intensification of militancy, the presence of the Indian army in Kashmir was gradually stepped up. On the one hand,

Kashmiri Pandits were made to leave by the machinations of Jagmohan, on the other the militants and the Indian army jointly affected the civic life in an adverse way., The linking of innocents to alleged anti-Indian and pro-Indian activities, irrespective of their religion, went up. Thus, the Kashmiri people were/are caught in the crossfire of militants and the Indian army and paramilitary personnel. The rising misery of people in the valley was worse confounded as the violation of Human Rights went up by leaps and bounds. The rehabilitation process of Pandits outside Kashmir and of the victims of militants and army in Kashmir was nowhere close to satisfactory. The militancy, which began initially due to alienation, was later on reinforced by the Al Qaeda terrorists, once they defeated the USSR armies in Afghanistan. There is a section of militants being trained in Pakistan. Pakistan has been presenting them as 'disgruntled' Kashmiris, who are fighting for the freedom of Kashmir. In 2002, Pervez Musharraf did agree that Pakistan will check the infiltration of the militants. Some of the Kashmiri leaders, like Yasin Malik who initially supported militancy as the solution to Kashmir's problem, are now talking of peaceful solution to the issue. India, even today, continues to press Pakistan to contain cross-border militants, to little avail.

The change of governments did not ease the repressive atmosphere created by the intervention of Indian army. The heartening thing in the whole process was the assembly elections of 2002, which were much more democratic than the earlier ones. Mufti Mohammad's government took positive steps in readiness to have dialogue with militants resulting in better situation. This was supplemented by better democratic norms than before, coming to the fore. The Kargil incident left the Indian government humiliated but thanks to the intervention of the White House, the temporary conflagration was over. The Agra summit was foiled by the Hindu Right Wingers, led by Lal Krishna Advani, who put his foot down and any semblance of a solution to the problem of people of Kashmir was put on hold.

The Problem

Kashmir has been treated as a piece of real estate by both India and Pakistan, and the aspiration of people of Kashmir have been the biggest casualty in the game. Both these countries have been very rigid in their approach to agree to a solution, which can bring peace. The things have been changing from last couple of years, when the local people are fed up totally due to the bloodbath in the valley.

India has been holding that as per the treaty of accession ratified by Kashmir assembly, whole Kashmir is a part of India. The UN assembly had asked for plebiscite but vacation of aggression by Pakistani army was the prerequisite for that. Within the country, Hindu right wing, RSS combine has been asking for the abolition of article 370 and the total merger of Kashmir into India like any other State. Different governments have taken the attitudes of going to the extent of granting autonomy but no such commitment has been actualised. As India is a secular state, it holds that the decision about Kashmir cannot be on religious grounds, the main argument put forward by Pakistan. Indian argument has been that Pakistan is using Kashmir for diversionary tactics, to keep the pot boiling. Pakistan has been suppressing its own diverse ethnicities, earlier Bengalees and now Balochs.

Pakistan's main argument has centered on the two nation theory, that majority of Kashmiris are Muslims so it should be part of Pakistan. This ignores the point that the Kashmiris never wanted to merge with Pakistan. Pakistan's argument is that India has not held plebiscite and that majority of Kashmiris would have opted for Pakistan. This is doubtful as many surveys have pointed out that Kashmiris do not want to merge with Pakistan, they would prefer an autonomous state. It is also argued by Pakistan that India is holding Kashmir on the gunpoint through its army. There is a suppression of Human rights of Muslims in India, which though in name is a secular State but in practice minorities are discriminated against. Interestingly though it is true that minorities are oppressed in India, the level of freedom in Indian part of Kashmir is more than in Azad Kashmir, held by Pakistan, a dictatorial State. The sore point in the whole argument is the role of Indian army in the state. Surely many in Kashmir do see it as an occupation army, the way it tramples on the human rights of the average Kashmiris. Many, especially from Pakistan, see the militants as children of Kashmiri fathers killed by the Indian security. True, the plight of such young people continues to be miserable.

Peaceful Solution

The solution to Kashmir's problems or better put, the problem of Kashmiri people, lies in expression of their aspirations, which have been suppressed since the very beginning of India as an independent country. Their suppression due to the policies of the central government resulted in their alienation and later to militancy. Kashmir being divided into two parts is a source of further complication. Pakistan, being a military dictatorship, off and on in the name Islam, is a source of further complication. How does one over come these? The role of the US in the whole process is also to be seen. USA had been the major protector of Pakistan, as Pakistan has been providing military bases and has been acting as its satellite in the east. It is only lately that the emphasis on peace talks has been growing. Half a century down the line, things are not the same as in 1947. In the mean time, over 50,000 innocent lives have been lost, Kashmiri pandits have left the valley due to various factors, and communal forces in India are making a political capital out of this. Pakistan is an important player in the game, as it set up terrorist bases for and on the instigation of the US to train Al Qaeda for aggression against the USSR armies in Afghanistan. The South Asian agenda of the US is still being fulfilled through Pakistan. So, today there are multiple players in the game.

The short-term measures of opening up travel between the two parts of Kashmir are a welcome development; making the borders more open and porous will depend on the stoppage of infiltration of terrorist. Within the Indian part of Kashmir, strengthening of democracy is the key to further solutions. It may not be a single-shot solution. It is felt that reduction in the number of armed forces is a must for any opening up of the democratic spaces.

The major options for Kashmiri people, battered economically, are the restoration of peace to begin with and later to go towards autonomy of Kashmir. Whether azadi or autonomy will remain is a matter of debate. It seems in the present circumstances, azadi (freedom) may be a far-fetched goal, which depends a lot on the attitude of Pakistan. Just by calling the Pakistan occupied Kashmir as Azad Kashmir has not given any democratic rights to Kashmiris living in that part of the country. The interconnection between the two Kashmirs will also remain a bone of contention. The ideal will be, to let democracy grow in both the parts of Kashmir, with porous borders and easy visa regimes.

What is within the reach of the Indian part of Kashmir on its own? As we have seen, the accession of Kashmir to India took place under a treaty of accession according to which Kashmir was to have its own constitution, its own Prime Minister and Sadr-e-Riyast. India was to have control on defense, external affairs, communication and currency. This is what the meaning of Article 370 was. Successive Indian governments have eroded most of the clauses of this article and even the remnant of these clauses is being aggressively opposed by the BJP. Autonomy does not mean separation from the Indian state; it only means respect of the accession treaty under which it acceded (not merged with India). Most of the free elections in Kashmir have seen the victory of a political party (National Conference), which has been advocating this autonomy. It reflects what the real aspirations of the people are. Even today in Kashmir, due to the alienation created by various factors some of the people still talk of azadi (independence). However, there have been a larger number of people who want to remain in India with a good deal of autonomy and devolution of power and empowerment of people. There is a need for dialogue with different groups and parties and accommodativeness to ensure that miseries of Kashmiris come to an end and Kashmiri pandits are able to return to their homes. Aggressive nationalism and pure assertions are no solution. Also Pakistan does not have its own game to play here; legally nor morally does Pakistan have any right to talk on behalf of Kashmiri people, as Pakistan itself has mostly been a dictatorship and does not reflect the aspirations of the people of Pakistan. There will be many obstacles in this path which require patience and respecting the wishes of the people.

With deepening of democratic space and democratic process, surely militancy will have no room, as at present. The increase in the number of armed personnel, which is a knee-jerk response to the violence in the valley, is no solution. If at all, it is actually counterproductive.

It is a pure coincidence that Kashmir has been caught up in the present global political chessboard. Being strategically important, the US has been backing Pakistan so far in its moves in this part of the world. Linking it up with the other reasons for terrorism is a clever move to undermine the deeper issues involved. One can say that the deeper issues which are resulting in terrorism are the Western politics for control of oil wealth, the rising communal assertiveness in India, and the Kashmir imbroglio. Overall the people of Kashmir should be allowed to take their own decision, the obstacles in the path are too many and they need to be overcome in a peaceful manner, with dialogue and removal of the bayonets pointing at the chests of people of Kashmir.

References

Praful Bidwai, Welcome move on Kashmir, *Rediff.com*, 29 April 2003.
Nehru Jawaharlal, *Collected Works,* Publications Division XVIII, 421.
Puri Balraj, *Kashmir: Towards Insurgency,* Orient Longman, 1993.
Sufi GMD, *Kashmir, Lahore1958 and Shrinagar 1977*, Vols I and II.

Politics over Paradise

India's freedom was accompanied by partition and the issue of Princely States. These States had Kings and Princes as sovereigns, who were given the choice to either merge with India or Pakistan, or to remain independent with many guidelines that had to be followed. At the time of independence, there were over five hundred small and big princely States.

While the problems of most of the States were solved with ease, the Princes of Hyderabad, Junagarh and Kashmir hesitated in taking any decision. Hyderabad and Junagarh were merged into India by military action. Kashmir's King Hari Singh wanted to remain independent and he had the vision of developing Kashmir into a Switzerland of Asia. He offered 'standstill' agreements to both India and Pakistan. While Pakistan accepted the treaty, India refused. Before any conclusive decision could be reached about the status of Kashmir, Pakistan invaded Kashmir, with its army disguised as tribals requesting the Indian the army to come to Kashmir to defend it. Nehru stated that unless some agreement is signed, India couldn't send its army to a State where it has no legal standing.

As pointed out above, a treaty of accession was drafted with Article 370 for safeguard of the people of the State. But from 1953 the Indian government started to supervise the affairs of Kashmir.

The major bones of contention are support to militants from the Pakistan, arming them and other logistic support. Al Qaeda also joined militancy in Kashmir at the turn of the century. Pakistan occupied Kashmir has been called Azad Kashmir. As Pakistan herself has military dictatorship, to call occupied Kashmir as Azad Kashmir is a travesty of truth. India's position has been to stick to the treaty of accession between Maharaja Hari Singh and the Indian government. The flaw on this side is that India has not stuck to the clause of autonomy and there is a heavy military presence in the State. Thus the people of Kashmir have been victims of militancy as well as the atrocities of the Indian army.

Two Kashmirs

So, instead of a Switzerland, now there are two Kashmirs. The Indian part of Kashmir is gradually started becoming normal for some time. One could see an actual decline in the acts of terror. Two problematic areas which worsened the situation in the times to come were:

a. Presence of military in civilian area.
b. The trade and travel route between the two Kashmir not being open.

While the Pakistan military and the civilian government has been harping on a rigid stance, the democratically elected Pakistan governments seems to be more amicable to a peaceful solution of the inter-state issue.

Terror Troubles

The formation of Al Qaeda resulted in many fall-outs in the Indian part of Kashmir over a period of time. As America propagated the word 'Islamic terrorism', Islam and Muslims got demonised as responsible for terrorism. In India, an already existing anti-Muslim propaganda led to the association of the Kashmir issue with separatist tendencies of Muslims, overlooking the real causes of the phenomenon. After the initial part played by Al Qaeda in Kashmir, Al Qaeda and like-minded groups also started their disruptive acts in other parts of India. With the prevalent notion of Islam=Muslims=Pakistan, the social common sense here worsened the image of Muslims. As such Al Qaeda had a different logic.

Hanging of Afzal Guru: Political Dilemmas

The semi-secretive hanging of Afzal Guru (Feb 2013) had come as a shock to some and as a feeling of triumph for many. Afzal Guru, a Kashmiri, was accused of complicity in the 2001 Parliament attack and was hanged in the early hours of 9 February 2013 and was supposedly buried in the prison yard. His mercy petition, which was pending with the President for long, was finally rejected and even before the family of Afzal Guru could get a chance to appeal against the turning down of clemency, Guru was hanged. While the ethical questions pertaining to death penalty are heavy on the conscience of many in India, this is not regarded as the part of 'collective conscience' which has guided the judgement of the Supreme Court and later the President, who turned down his petition for clemency. The section of society which thought that Guru's sentence itself needed to be questioned, also does not seem to form the 'conscience' of the nation!

In February 2013, Kashmir valley was totally insulated from news, and TV channels were gagged. The restive mood of the people led to protests and deaths. In the absence of the proper information, rumours did the rounds and what disastrous consequences such rumours can have needs a serious thought from the rulers in the corridors of power in India. This hanging raised many questions. Why hanging and why at that particular time? Guru was one of the accused in the case of assault on the Parliament. Guru was not found to be part of any terrorist outfit, nor did he play any direct role in this attack. In the trial which took place, the provisions of the International Covenant on Civil and Political Rights was NOT respected. The Supreme Court of India noted that there was no direct evidence of Gurus' involvement. The evidence was mainly circumstantial. All three courts, including the apext court, had acquitted him of the charges under POTA of belonging to either a terrorist organisation or a terrorist gang. Courts also noted that the evidence against Guru was fabricated. The police had lied about the time and place of arrest, fabricated evidence including arrest memos and extracted false confessions. The petition by social activists and acedemics points out, 'The fact that the Court appointed as amicus curiae (friend of the court) a lawyer in whom Afzal had expressed no faith; the fact that he went legally unrepresented from the time of his arrest till his so-called confession, the fact that the Court asked him to either accept the lawyer appointed by the Court or cross examine the witness himself should surely have concerned you while considering his mercy petition.'

At best, Guru was a facilitator in the crime (just like the Lankan and Indian Tamil accused of complicity in Rajiv Gandhi's murder) and not a direct perpetrator of the crime.

His personal history of being a surrendered militant, of harassment and torture at the hands of the Special Task Force, as well as his statement in open court that he had indeed helped Mohammad, one of the attackers on the Parliament, find a house and obtain a car, the same car used in the attack, but at the orders of his STF handlers, should have spurred a full-scale investigation into the allegations. The citizens of this country do not know if one was ordered at all.

Court noted that Guru was not a member of any banned organisation, Court ruled, 'The conviction under section 3 (2) of POTA is set aside. The conviction under section 3 (5) of POTA is also set aside because there is no evidence that he is a member of a terrorist organisation, once the confessional statement is excluded. Incidentally, we may mention that even going by confessional statement, it is doubtful whether the membership of a terrorist gang or organisation is established.' Further, it noted, since 'The incident, which resulted in heavy casualties, had shaken the entire nation and the collective conscience of the society will only be satisfied if capital punishment is awarded to the offender.' So does it mean that the punishment is being given to assuage the collective national conscience? One must add, what was presented as this 'conscience' was the consciousness of a section of dominant middle classes and assertive social-political groups in particular. The 'conscience' manufactured by the likes of the VHP, Bajrang Dal and company, have come to be labelled and accepted as national collective conscience by many. It is these groups who celebrated Afzal Guru's death, exhibiting their triumph. The basis on which Supreme Court gave its judgment was built by the police, with methods which are questionable, which the court has reprimanded in this case. The argument on the other side was that if Guru was not hanged it would be an insult to those who laid down their lives for defending the parliament.

While Supreme Court deserves all the respect, one has to see that the primary investigation done by the police, with all its flaws formed the base of the judgment. When that investigation itself had holes in it, should it have been accepted at all by the highest court in the country, in the form it was presented? When the primary culprits are either dead are some of them absconding, can 'the whole truth be out'? Or is it that somebody has anyway to be punished to quench the thirst for revenge, and who better than the one who has a Muslim name and happens to be from Kashmir? The whole trial of Afzal needed to be revisited; the flaws of the investigation, the weakness of and deliberate violation of norms by the police and authorities in particular.

Now come the question as to why Rajiv Gandhi's alleged assassins and Punjab Chief Minister Beant Singh's killers are being given a different treatment? The assemblies of Punjab and Tamil Nadu have passed resolutions against death penalties for these people, who were directly involved with the acts of assassination. The whole issue boils down to how the Indian state has treated the Kashmir issue and how terrorism and Muslims have been associated in the popular thinking. This thinking has been deliberately promoted by the communal forces in the country. A section of the media has played a very negative role in promoting such divisive thinking in society. Sections of media have acted as spokespersons for the police versions of the investigation. So the 'collective conscience' is the common desire asserted by communal forces. It does reflect the state of our democracy overall. Can we call ourselves as a democracy and indulge in minority bashing and be high handed in matters of justice and citizenship rights in cases of the vulnerable minorities.

Kashmir had been limping towards a better situation during the last few years. While alienation amongst large sections of Kashmiris remains deep set, there have been indications that people may reconcile to the situation, if the democratisation process in Kashmir is strengthened by and by. This hanging of Afzal Guru reminds one of the hanging of Maqbul Butt in 1984, which set the trail for a phase of militancy.

We also need to take the issue of protests in Kashmir in a more balanced way. Unfortunately, the Congress hunts with the hound and runs with the hare in this game of aggressive jingoism. Such cases of yielding to religious nationalism will surely be a recipe for disaster for the process of normalisation in Kashmir. It will be like actively associating with the divisive ideology.

Land Allotment and Amarnath Shrine

Jammu and Kashmir has been one of the regions of the country mired in different types of troubles all through. To add to the painful situation, the issue of land allotment to Amarnath shrine and later, a reversal of this decision, has worsened the harmony, which is eluding the region.

The J&K government, in contravention to a Supreme Court ruling, decided to divert 39.88 (June 2008) hectares of land to the Amarnath Shrine Board (SASB). This was preceded by a lot of miscalculations and misrepresentations. In the volatile situation of the State, this land diversion was presented as if the land was sold to the Shrine Board. This meant also changing the tourism-related services in the State. Traditionally, the economic activity generated due to the pilgrimage or Amarnath yatra is one of the major sources of income for Muslims en-route. With SASB taking over many/all these services, a perception was created that those regularly associated with the yatra services will be sidetracked and it will now become an exclusively Hindu affair. Further, this was wrongly perceived in the valley as an attempt to change the demographic profile of J&K by settling more Hindus in the region. This baseless perception had some roots in the common knowledge that Shimon Peres, the Israeli Foreign Minister, had advised Lal Krishna Advani about changing the demographic composition in the valley. These twin factors were in the minds of people when this land diversion was presented as the 'sale of land' and spontaneously there were huge protests in the valley. Separatist extremist sections of Kashmir's politicians, fueled the fire of protests and were immediately projected as anti-national by the BJP etc and huge anti-protest demonstrations were orchestrated in the Jammu region.

The Amaranth yatra by Hindus is rooted in one of the most syncretic-mixed support structures. The cave where the shrine is located was the discovery of a Muslim shepherd in the 1850s, since when a pilgrim to the cave began. The descendents of the Muslim shepherd and sadhus managed the yatra till 2001, when the SASB took over and is trying to increase its hold on the arrangements. Remarkably, the yatra went on smoothly even at the peak of militancy in Kashmir, barring, of course, a few aberrations here and there. Then, in 2006, the then Governor ordered the placing of dry ice on the Lingam (phallus, the holy deity) which showed signs of melting due to the increase in atmospheric temperature caused by increase in the yatra traffic and unseasonal heat. This was also a matter of protests. The pilgrimage is the major annual tourist event for the whole State, a means of bread butter for many of them. Also the syncretism in people's attitude is explicit all through as one sees the deep interconnection of the religious communities in the organisation and carrying out of the yatra logistics. This again came to the fore when the pilgrims who got trapped due to breaking out of the demonstrations were well served by the Muslims en-route, who organised the food supplies and other assisstance to them.

The spontaneous breaking out of protest in the valley was used by elements like Syed Ali Shah Gilani, belonging to the extremist faction of the Hurriat Conference in the valley politics, who went on to fan the fire of separatism during the agitations and further aggravated the situation by calling for boycott of polls to be held that October.

The ruling coalition of Congress and the regional PDP were far from objective. Both the coalition partners calculated more in terms of vote bank rather than going by the ethos of democratic and secular values. Congress forced the diversion of the land under pressure from Governor Sinha, and the PDP, sensing the mood in the valley backed out, leading the government to revert the order. Consequently, the PDP walked out of the coalition, leading to the fall of the government.

In Jammu region, the BJP and its allies had inflamed the situation by organising massive bandhs. Its call for an all-India Bandh led to many highhanded actions, more so in BJP ruled States, the worst of which was death of several people in Indore, Madhya Pradesh due to the accompanying violence. In J&K too the atmosphere was communalised. Contrary to local feelings, it has also been talking of trifurcating of J&K, along religious lines—Kashmir valley, Jammu and Ladhakh. Demanding of separate statehood for Jammu was one of the causes of electoral defeat of the BJP in the 2001 elections.

Politicising the Plight of Kashmiri Pandits

The wholesale migration of Pandits from the valley was a big blow to the traditions of the valley. As the figures above show, the damage by militants is to both the communities and not to Hindus alone. The Pandits had considered migration first in 1986 but this decision was held in abeyance due to the appeals of a goodwill mission, which was constituted by reputed Kashmiris, steeped in plural culture. In 1990 the militancy was stepped up. This time around, Jagmohan, the hard core right winger, was the Governor of Kashmir and he ensured dissolution of the goodwill mission to Pandits by pressurising one of the Pandit members of the team to migrate to Jammu (Puri, 2000, 65). Balraj Puri in March 1990 stated, 'I found no hostility among common Muslims in Kashmir against Pandits, and that allegations of gross violations of Human rights by security forces needs to be investigated (Puri, 2000, 66).' At that time, Hindu communal forces took it upon themselves to spread fear and terror amongst Pandits, 'Much disinformation is being spread in Jammu and Delhi that scores of Hindu temples and shrines have been desecrated or destroyed in Kashmir. This is completely untrue and it is baffling that the government has not thought it fit to ask Doordarshan to do a programme on mandirs in Kashmir, just to reassure people that they remain unharmed. (Press Council of India, 1991.)'

There is no doubt that the problem of Pandits' migration out of the Kashmir valley is an unfortunate outcome of the alienation of Kashmiri people, resulting in militancy. The role of external terrorists was most disastrous in precipitating the exodus of Pandits. Another factor has been due to result of Hindu communalist outfits' baseless spreading of fear psychosis and there was added pressure from Governor Jagmohan and not due to any Hindu-Muslim hostility.

Politics is a strange game where no holds are barred for electoral advantages. It also expresses, to some extent, the political ideology of those playing these games in addition to the distortion of events, which are done deliberately. Interpretation of the very same events is diametrically different for different political groups. The exodus of Kashmiri Pandits, thus meant diferent things to different political dispensatons.

During his election campaign, Narendra Modi too made several statements on Kashmir which were factually inaccurate and could be interpreted as communal. He said that the biggest blow to secular fabric of India was delivered from Kashmir, from where Kashmiri Pandits were forced out and that the Abdullahs (Sheikh Abdulla, Farooq and Omar) were behind it (28th April 2014). In response, Farooq and Omar shot back that exodus of Pandits took place under the President's Rule with Jagmohan, a BJP hand, as the Governor of Kashmir. A part of the time, it was the VP Singh government in power, supported by the BJP from the outside. While all three Addullahs are not the same, nor is their role a continuum, nor all of them secular angels, the exodus of Pandits is much more complex than that being attributed to them. The role which each of the Abdullas played cannot be put in the same basket.

As such, communalism has been the great bane of the subcontinent and its biggest and most tragic expression was the partition of India in which millions were butchered and a larger number migrated to both sides of the border. Apart from these migrations which took place, forcing people to far off lands, there are local migrations also, which took place in the aftermath of communal violence of mass scale, like the one in Mumbai 1992-93 or Gujarat 2002 where thousand of people left their homes, where they were living for decades and shifted to the other parts of the same city leading to formation of ghettoes, Mumbra in

Mumbai and Juhapura in Ahmadabad being two major examples. Incidentally, the Hindu population in Kashmir had gone through a very complex history of conversion to Buddhism and later to Islam through Sufi saints. The Hindus started being referred to as Pandits from 15th Century onwards. This happened after Akbar won over Kashmir and employed the Hindus in his administration. He was impressed by their qualities and conferred the title Pandit on them.

The first major exodus of Pandits took place after the partition riots and partly due to land reforms introduced by Sheikh Abdullah.

The roots of the later exodus of Kashmiri Pandits lie in the decision of the Maharaja of Kashmir to remain independent. This was followed by the attack of the Kabayilis from Pakistan and Sheikh Abdullah's decision to accede with India and not with Pakistan. This decision was not on religious considerations but was with the hope that in India secularism will flourish with leaders like Gandhi and Nehru. In 1948 Gandhi was killed by communal forces. Just to recall, Article 370 was the basis of accession of Kashmir to India. This Article gave autonomy to Kashmir Assembly in most matters. With the opposition to this clause and demand for forcible merger of Kashmir to India by communal forces, Kasmiris lost their faith in India's intentions. With Abdullah's arrest began the process of alienation in Kashmir. This process of alienation led to militancy. With encouragement from Pakistan, it took on dangerous proportions. Still this militancy was centered on the concept of Kashmiriyat. Kashmiriyat is synthesis of Buddhism, Vedanta and Sufi traditions. After the hanging of Maqbool Butt in 1985, Al Qaeda type elements became active in Kashmir. Soon this militancy got transformed to being communal politics. The result was that the Hindus, the Pandits, started being targeted.

The process of the latest exodus in the 1990s began with communalisation of the militancy, a transition from Kashmiriyat to that of the Muslim. One version a la Modi says that Kashmiri Pandits were driven from Kashmir valley by the Muslim militants and this was a planned move by Muslim majority Kashmir. Fact is, the Muslim majority was totally opposed to the harassment of Pandits.

In this militancy, while Hindus were targeted in a big way, even Muslims were not spared.

The wholesale migration of Pandits from the valley was a big blow to the traditions of the valley. The damage by militants was to both the communities and not to Hindus alone. The Pandits were intimidated much more and had considered migration first in 1986, but this decision was held in abeyance due to the appeals of a goodwill mission, which was constituted by reputed Kashmiris, steeped in plural culture. As we saw, in 1990 militancy was stepped up. This time around Jagmohan, who later became a minister in the BJP-led NDA government, was the Governor of Kashmir.

All things considered, the problem of Pandits migration is unfortunate outcome of the alienation of Kashmiri people and surely not due to the Abdullahs. By selectively harping on the plight of Kashmiri Pandits while the other victims of violence in Kashmir are totally left out of their scheme of propaganda, communal forces are only encouraging disquiet in Kashmir. The BJP led NDA rules have hardly done anything different to improve the lop-sided policies of the earlier governments of India and for the victims of militancy.

Poet Kalhan of Kashmir, in his classic *Rajtarangini* writes that it is only through punya (noble deeds) and not force that Kashmir can be won over. We need to remind ourselves of this profound advice from Kalhan while making policies about Kashmir. Rather than putting the blame on one political stream, the role of global politics, the historical baggage of partition and post-partition problems, the role of global terrorism, its influence on militancy in Kashmir and the role of communal forces in spreading fear also need to be kept in mind while commenting on this tragedy of mammoth proportions.

Kashmiriyat Revisited

On 18 June 2010, nearly a thousand Kashmiri Pandits, including women and children, visited the temple of Mata Kheer Bhavani in Tullamula, 20 kilometers from Srinagar. It was the sacred day of Zyeshtha Ashthami. Most of them were visiting the valley after nearly 20 years, since the time they left Kashmir due to various reasons like militancy and the way migration was handled by the authorities. The spiritual zest to worship the Goddess, Ragnya Devi, to whom this temple is dedicated, was in the air. There was a big congregation of local Muslims who greeted the visiting pandits with cold drinks and kheer (a dessert made of milk and rice). The Kashmir CM, Farooq Abdullah, and many other Kashmir Ministers also turned up for this emotional occasion marked by reunion with many a visiting Pandit.

The local Muslims and the ministers said that all concerned should work for return of the Pandits to the valley, as Kashmiriyat is incomplete without the Pandits, who are an integral part of Kashmir's culture and life. Many a Pandit also promised to work towards such a goal, to overcome the divides created by the militant and political forces. Since then began a trickle of returning Pandits to the valley.

Kashmir has been seen by the two neighbours, Pakistan and India, more as an issue of 'real estate' only. Kashmir has been treated as a 'territory' which has to be won over by any means. The government of Pakistan has regularly used the 'Kashmir' issue to retain its hold on the political power in Kashmir, while in India, for far too long the central government has ignored the aspirations of the local population. In this whole scenario the real essence of Kashmir and Kashmiriyat has got undermined.

The soul of Kashmir's culture has been a close interaction between different religious traditions, teachings of Buddha, Vedanta and Sufi tradition of Islam. Kashmir was the place where Buddhism spread far and wide and most of the population, except the upper caste, embraced Buddhism. With attacks on Buddhism in the 8th Century, the tide turned. Later many Sufis came to Kashmir and preached their version of Islam. The most famous of them has been Nooruddin Noorani, popularly known as Nund Rishi. He was influenced by Lal Dedh, who herself was influenced by the earlier Sufis. Her mystical verses have Shaivite syntax. Today both Hindus and Muslims regard her as their own. Like the great Bhakti saint, Kabir, there is a story that when Lal Dedh died her body turned into a heap of flowers, half of which were consigned to flames by Hindus, while the remaining half was buried by Muslims.

Nund Rishi wrote in appreciation of Lal Dedh, about her syncretic spiritual values which taught that one should not differentiate between a Hindu and a Muslim, one should realise one's own self and that's what God is. On Similar lines, Nund Rishi focused on purification of soul. He bitterly criticised mullahs and Brahmins, whose focus was more on rituals than on spirituality and morality. Nund Rishi's was a sort of mass movement in Kashmir, which affected many Kashmiris and they embraced Islam as taught by him. This reflects the rich syncretic culture of Kashmir, evolved over years and under threat from present political scenario.

Kashmir in Turmoil 2016

Turmoil in Kashmir has been a very major matter of concern for the last many decades. While grim situations have occurred earlier also, the one witnessed in July 2016 is as serious as the one witnessed after the arrest of Sheikh Abdullah in 1953. The toll in the mounting agitation has been over 75 dead, nearly 9,000 injured, over a hundred of them fully or partly blinded. The armed forces used pellet guns to suppress the upsurge. In 2016, Kashmir witnessed the longest ever period of curfew in the last two decades. As is well known, this unrest was precipitated by the killing of Burhan Wani, a young Hurriyat commander. He was a very popular figure among the youth for his regular social media postings.

The Incident

Half an hour after his death, the Indian media erupted in celebration, announcing victory. The media on twitter and television continued to gloat. '…Burhan Wani elimination BIG NEWS', tweeted Barkha Dutt of *NDTV*. Abhijit Majumdar, the managing editor of *Mail Today* wrote, 'With Burhan Wani's killing, Indian forces have eliminated entire gang of Facebook terror poster-boys of #Kashmir one after the other. Salute.' It was reported that the entire Valley descended in gloom and it began to rain incessantly. In Srinagar, cars, trucks, motorcycles and other automobiles began to honk mindlessly.[1]

The perceptions in major parts of Kashmir were very different and well reflected by writer Bashrat Ali: 'As the entire Valley shut down in mourning—protests, stone-pelting, congregational funeral prayers—people began to count the dead. The numbers kept rising. The protest demonstrations kept swelling. The campaign of killing, blinding, maiming and torturing of people continued. The Indian state and the constructed rivals within Jammu and Kashmir lost all the ground ...'[2]

There are questions aplenty as to why pellet guns are used only in Kashmir? Does it not reflect the treatment meted out to Kashmiris? The casualties, deaths and injuries had started mounting in July 2016 and this was met by more strong action from the side of state.

The State and Kashmir Policies

The central government is making policies in Kashmir on the basis of its understanding that it is Pakistan which is instigating the Kashmiri youth to protest and throw stones. An interesting story in *Outlook* magazine points out that youth are totally disgusted with the treatment they have been receiving, 'They laugh off suggestion that they are paid money by separatists to pelt stones and that Pakistan and its secret agency ISI is behind them.'[3]. As per this report, religion is not a factor in their understanding of the situation in Kashmir.

After the latest round of unrest broke out, for a long time there was no conciliatory measure from the central government. The Home Minister of India, Rajnath Singh, visited the Valley and then led a 29-member parliamentary delegation to the Valley but the dissatisfaction remained. His list of those whom he was to meet did not have the names of Hurriyat leaders. BJP leaders including Rajnath Singh have all spoken against any dialogue with the Hurriyat leaders.[4]

Later, some opposition leaders tried to meet some of the Hurriyat leaders. The analysis of the government has been that the protesters are merely a small part of the population; five per cent or so. They are being prompted and funded by the Pakistan government, according to the government of India. This interpretation cannot be validated by ground realities. Such a large surge of people cannot be instigated by foreign forces, though foreign forces do put oil in the fire. The deeper disgust and anguish of the people is not in the calculation of the state.

The separatist elements have been becoming stronger over a period of time and more or less continuously. Ever since the hanging of Maqbul Butt, incidents of militant activities against Kashmiri Pandits, the hanging of Afzal Guru and the rape of girls in Shopian (2013) by army personnel gave grist to the mill of pro-Pakistan sentiments. These are growing and becoming stronger by the day. The refusal of Syed Ali Shah Gilani to meet the leaders of the all-party delegation who called upon him, also show the hardening stance of some of them. While the call for azadi (freedom) is a regular cry, we must keep in mind that the pro-Pakistan sentiments are also growing in intensity.

Rajesh Rajdan and Ajya Raina (*Scroll.in*) point out, 'SAR Geelani, one of the leading and unwavering advocates of Jammu and Kashmir's secession, is also a long-standing central pillar of Jamaat-e-Islami Kashmir. To its credit, Jamaat-e-Islami has never made any bones about it being an Islamist organisation that advocates Kashmir's merger with Pakistan on the basis of Islamic faith followed by majority of people in Kashmir... The fig leaf of azadi blows away every time Narae-e-takbir, Allah hu Akbar reverberates in a secessionist rally in Kashmir. Allow us to translate it for you – "Shout out the phrase, Allah-is-Great". This phrase has its rightful place amongst the believers in a mosque, but when it is shouted in every secessionist rally, no amount of obfuscation can hide the truth that for secessionists, azadi from secular India is in the name of Islamic faith of Kashmir's Muslims.'[5]

Role of Pakistan

The BJP led coalition at the center looks at the Kashmir issue as an issue of land, that's what the ultranationalists do. The discomfort in the people's minds; disgust due to violation of the clauses of autonomy in particular are nowhere in the consideration of this government. The role of Pakistan in worsening the crisis is very clear. Pakistan has been encouraging the alienated youth since way back in the 1950s. Currently, Pakistan has been making loud noises about the violation of human rights in Kashmir and making all efforts to internationalise the issue. It sent many of its leaders to different World capitals to apprise other countries about the Kashmir issue. There is a demand that the international tribunal should investigate the killings in Kashmir. Many leaders from Pakistan are worsening the crisis by sending encouraging signals to the protesters. Hafiz Sayeed, for example, urged the Pakistan army to send forces into Kashmir.[6] Pakistan's position is that Kashmir being a Muslim majority State should be part of Pakistan and people of Kashmir should be part of talks between Pakistan and India.

As such, one of the bones of contention is the Armed Forces Special Powers Act which grants immunity against legal action against the armed forces personnelle. These men are dime a dozen in the region, estimated to be around six hundred thousand. They have been stationed in civilian areas for years. Last few decades have seen a worsening scenario in Kashmir and the unrest has been dealt with by increasing the number of troops in the Valley.

Frustrated Youth of Kashmir

The sentiments of Kashmiri youth have been on display time and over again. The last major turmoil was on the issue of a Cricket match when West Indies defeated India (April 2016). The local students celebrated when India got defeated in the World T20 match. This went on to create a ruckus between the local Kashmiri students and those who are outsiders to Kashmir and are in majority. These majority non-Kashmiri students and locals showed a clear divide. The outsiders were forcing others to shout Bharat Mata Ki Jai. (Hail mother India.) Accoding to media reports, 'The non-local students also allegedly shouted anti-Kashmir and other inflammatory slogans, and burnt the national flag of Pakistan. Fearing clashes, the administration closed the institute (NIT) for the weekend and ordered students to vacate the hostel. The vacation order was, however, revoked in the evening. On Monday, the institute opened normally as calm returned and classes resumed. However, a group of non-local students, seeking action against Kashmiri students, organised a protest, shouting inflammatory slogans, and keeping the campus (NIT) on the edge. Clashes erupted again when they tried to take out a rally on Tuesday and were stopped.'[7]

The media reports continued, 'In the wake of the NIT crisis in the Kashmir valley, many officers of J&K Police found themselves caught between a rock and a hard place. On the one hand, the police are disaraged as "collaborators" and "killers" by the local population for fighting the popular indigenous militancy. On the other, New Delhi just made obvious its distrust of the police – or so the officers believe – by replacing them with the paramilitary to provide security at the NIT.'[8]

The clear-cut divide between the local sentiments and the Indian nationalist sentiments of those who are not from Kashmir was most evident here. The local police was also soft towards local students and the outsiders demanded that NIT be moved away from Kashmir.

The role of media in alienating the people of Kashmir is also a major factor in the problems. 'In Kashmir, people often confuse the outrageous editorial policy of the national media with the oppressive State policy. When Kashmiri representatives are bullied in TV debates, their aspirations ridiculed, their grievances shouted down, the symbols of Kashmiri pride insulted, or when non-issues are given precedence over the killing of the innocents, when military bravado is encouraged over civilian agony, when positive initiatives of the State government are overlooked, and truth is not shown at all, and most importantly, when cows are made to feel more important than the Kashmiri people, the frustration and anger will, expectedly, be directed against India. Every hour of prime time TV news aggression pushes Kashmir a mile westward from India', says one writer. [9]

Time and time again while interacting with the youth from Kashmir what comes forth and gets highlighted is the pain and anguish of the youth, their frustration; their realisation about the brutality of the system in which they live in Kashmir. Youth from Kashmir coming to different parts of India for various meetings and interactions generally display a high level of understanding of the issues involved. The Kashmiri youth and students studying in different parts of India are vocal about the restlessness over their present and future. 'What have we done to be labeled as terrorists?' is one of the questions on their mind and lips. 'Why do we in Kashmir have to face torture from different quarters, including from the Indian army?' is another oft-repeated question. The restlessness is so much on display that one can gauge the depth of their feeling about the role of armed players, the militants and the Indian army, all in different measures.

The Interlocutors

What are the causes of the frustration of the youth and others from Kashmir and what is the way out? The last major attempt to understand the issue was the formation of a group of interlocutors in May 2012. The recommendations of the group of interlocutors, Dileep Padgaonkar, Radha Kumar and MM Ansari, were made public.[10] The then UPA government remained non-committal about this panel's recommendations, while the BJP rejected them on the ground that it is a dilution of the conditions of accession of Kashmir to India. The separatists find it insufficient, saying that there is no political settlement of the issue. Essentially, while the interlocutor's team has rejected the return to the pre-1953 position, it made significant recommendations which are in the direction of restoring the autonomy of Kashmir. Being close to the pre-1953 position, the team suggested that parliament will not make any law for Kashmir unless it relates to the security, internal and external of the State. Significantly, it gives the status of 'special' instead of 'temporary' to Article 370, which is the bone of contention for ultranationalists like the BJP. Very correctly, the team has said that the proportion of officers in the State should gradually be changed to increase the prominence and role of the local officers. It also talked of creating regional councils with financial powers, and measures to promote cooperation across the Line of Control (LoC). They also suggested resumption of dialogue with the Hurriyat and Pakistan, both.

The team had done its homework quite well and while addressing the issue of discontent in J&K, they also tried to register the realities which have emerged during the last six decades. It has been a major effort around which debates for initiative were very much needed to restore the calm in the State. Undoubtedly, the people of Kashmir have suffered a severe violation of their human rights all through. The treaty of accession giving full autonomy to J&K has come under heavy strain from the communal forces in India right from the beginning, sowing the seeds of the problem in Kashmir.

Path to Peace

Today the major obstacle to the normal growth of the State is the conversion of the civilian areas into military barracks, army breathing down the necks of civilians all over. In India, the communal forces have projected this as another Hindu-Muslim issue. An issue with purely regional ethnic character came to be looked at through the prism of religion, adding to the misery of the Muslim population. As per the report of interlocutors, what we need utmost is proactive peace in the region and this peace can only begin with the internal withdrawal of military, supplemented by a process of dialogue with dissidents and Pakistan. Kashmir has been looked at as a real-estate issue by India and Pakistan both. The people of Kashmir need to be given primacy while thinking of a solution to the vexed issue affecting their peace. What we need to keep uppermost in our mind while discussing the recommendations of interlocutors is that, will these recommendations reduce the anguish of Kashmiri people in general and Kashmiri youth in particular? Nearly two generations of Kashmiri youth have suffered at the hands of the military and militants. The US-Pakistan nexus has also been a major player in spoiling the broth. A healthy debate around this report can be a good starting point to restore peace in the region.

Now the need for talks is more than before. Sajad Padder correctly points out, 'A parallel engagement on both tracks, New Delhi-Srinagar and New Delhi-Islamabad, is the need of the hour. Experiences show that whenever India-Pakistan relations improved, peace prevailed in Kashmir.[11] India must then seek to accommodate Kashmir with an autonomy that will satisfy the aspirations nurtured by this long period of revolt. Mohan Guruswamy, in a very perceptive article, points out 'With accession to Pakistan or a complete independence not being options, an acceptable via media must be and can be found. The breakthrough for that must happen in the minds of the rest of India. The heavens are not going to fall if Kashmir becomes an autonomous region within India. The extent of autonomy then becomes the only matter for discussion. We can afford to be generous. But is India ready for it?' [12]

This is a very crucial period for Indian secularism and people of Kashmir. The government seems to be toeing a hard line which has the risk of alienating the people further. This is most undesirable. Many a leadership of army posted in Kashmir, out of the experience of long engagement; also feel the need for dialogue with all stake holders.[13] Strengthening of democratic process in Kashmir is the crux of the matter and urgency in this direction is what is needed to be done by Indian state.

Footnotes

1. http://raiot.in/stories-indias-kashmir-experts-dont-tell/
2. http://raiot.in/stories-indias-kashmir-experts-dont-tell/
3. Showkatt A. Motta, Armed with Original Weapon, (Outlook 12 Sept 2016)
4. http://www.thecitizen.in/index.php/NewsDetail/index/1/8633/There-Is-An-India-That-Is-Not-the-BJP-Opposition-MPs-Defy-Govt-Meet-Mirwaiz-Yasin-Malik
5. http://scroll.in/article/804058/dear-ravish-kumar-you-brilliantly-made-visible-the-darkness-on-tv-but-you-got-one-detail-wrong
6. http://www.tribuneindia.com/news/nation/send-troops-to-kashmir-to-teach-india-lesson--hafiz-saeed-tells-pakistan/281020.html
7. https://www.thequint.com/politics/2016/04/07/how-a-cricket-match-brought-about-a-crisis-in-nit-srinagar
8. Gowher Gilani https://www.sabrangindia.in/article/%E2%80%98patriotic%E2%80%99-bjp-turns-nit-campus-cantonment-srinagar
9. Shah Faesal http://indianexpress.com/article/opinion/columns/kashmir-protest-burhan-wani-killing-selective-

indian-media-coverage-insensitive-residents-column-2922176/

10. http://www.firstpost.com/india/full-text-centres-interlocutors-report-on-jammu-and-kashmir-319954.html
11. I.E. Sept 13th, 2016, Mumbai
12. http://scroll.in/article/814274/for-azadi-for-all-it-ishttp-cms-scroll-team-time-to-break-the-fiction-of-jammu-and-kashmir
13. http://newsclick.in/army-has-spoken-kashmir-government-listening

Book Reviews

The Ghost of Two Nation Theory

(From web http://insaf.net/pipermail/sacw_insaf.net/2002/001367.html)

(Book Reviewed done in 2002: *Competing Nationalisms in South Asia, Essays for Asghar Ali Engineer*, Editors-Paul Brass and Achin Vanaik, Orient Longman, Hydrabad, Pages-298, Price Rs 525)

It is over five decades that most of the countries of South Asia got Independence from the clutches of colonial powers. During the struggle for Independence, two contrasting notions of nationalism emerged mainly due to lack of land reforms and incomplete secularisation process. As the period of freedom in most of these has not brought in social transformation towards Liberty, Equality and Fraternity in a substantial way, the ghost of the rabid phase of the conflict-ridden period of the 'two nation theory' has resurfaced in a stronger way again. It is in this backdrop that the book under review takes up the theme of the struggle between these two contrary concepts of nationalism. Brass and Vanaik have taken into consideration many facets of the problem and most of the essays by renowned contributors do justice to the themes being dealt with.

This is probably the most apt theme for the festschrift for Asghar Ali Engineer. Engineer is a pioneer in investigations of Communal Riots, and for human rights and secular values; he is also a major contributor to Bohra reforms. The last aspect, though a very important component of the corpus of Engineer's work, has not been touched upon, leaving a feeling of void in the volume dedicated to this outstanding activist scholar, who is probably the best known scholar on the subject of communal riots at a popular level. While the editorial does touch upon this aspect of his work, this does not form the theme. As such Asghar Ali Engineer must be amongst the foremost activists who realised the dangers of communal politics and took it up in right ernest as the major field of his activity. Starting as early as from the 1963 Jabalpur riots, he went on to investigate most of the major riots in India and set the pattern for riot investigation. His insights into the dynamics of communal violence helped him to formulate the theories and analyse the pattern of all such riots. From that time on, this professionally-trained engineer took to contributing to understanding the deeper malady of communal politics and his prolific pen poured out a mammoth oeuvre, which itself is a matter of study by university scholars now. He has also formed different organisations for Bohra reforms, study of Islam and secularism. As long as he lived, one could read at least three of his periodical contributions, two on secular issues and one on Islam, every month with a regularity, which beat many a lazy clock. His commitment to the cause and infinite stamina of work is a matter of great adulation of all those who have had the privilege to see him working from close quarters.

The editors of the volume in a way approve the spectrum of Engineer's work when they write, 'The struggle against communalism then, operates on a broad front and is inseparable from the struggle for greater democracy, social justice and better and more humane forms of material existence.' (p 4) The editors see the fascist nature of the Sangh Parivar, the core of Hindu communal organisations modeled on European Fascist movements. Their observation is more than vindicated when one goes through the pain and agony of current Gujarat (March-June 2002) as reflected in most of the reports of Human rights activists. Editors correctly point out the ideological predilection of the RSS towards the Brahminical values of caste and gender hierarchy. Of course, this notion of birth-based stratification is couched in most polished tones, the tone that sidetracks the values of Liberty, Equality and Fraternity with the clear agenda, the agenda of upholding the pre-modern feudal hierarchies, in the modern language. Since the lip service has to be paid to democracy and secularism, so new meanings and content is given to both the terms which cannot be formally rejected and comes the notions of cultural nationalism etc. in place of civic and democratic nationalism.

The volume editors do summarise the RSS and its philosophy and politics. But a volume devoted to the competing nationalisms in India cannot afford to leave out detailed treatment of the fountainhead of communal politics in India. This organisation, which operated silently till 80s and not many of its ideologues and leaders were known to the public, now has a series of 'spokesmen' whose job is to keep the media apprised of its decisions about various aspects of its politics. This is something, which this organisation has introduced, in the recent past to build its image in the media. It is also the indicator of the prowess of the organisation during the last decade. So far not many were aware that it is the RSS, which is at the back of all Hindutva organisations like te BJP, VHP, Bajarang Dal, Adivasi Kalyan Ashram etc. but now the connections are in the open. The fact that these organisations are under the ideological and functional control of RSS is fairly well known by now. A bit of organisational control, if needed, is exercised through the Swayamsevaks who form the controlling core of most of these organisations.

Though most of the essays of the volume are illuminating, the ones by Sikata Bannerjee, Anwar Alam, Ghnashyam Shah and Mubarak Ali do take the cake for raising many issues for introspection and serious thought. Bannerjee's article in a way is the theme of the volume as such. The contrasting notions of 'Nationalism' are civic and cultural. By civic nationalism one means the nationalism, which stands for secularism and democracy, the one, which takes citizenship as the primary focus of one's identity. In contrast, cultural nationalism draws from the elite's culture, regards the country as a cultural monolith, and is imposing in its approach towards minorities. Cultural nationalism is the elegant name for Hindu nationalism, Hindutva, the content of which is filled by its proponents. They claim that it is an alternative to secular nationalism in the Indian context but its values are those of the one's coming from the Brahminical streams. It has no place for subaltern religious traditions, the traditions that opposed the hegemonic Brahminical traditions. Banerjee points out the degeneration and compromise of the Congress party with communal outfits like the Shiv Sena at the local level. She is highly critical of the practices of the Congress at the grass roots level. She aptly sums up the claims of the practitioners of the two types of nationalisms: 'Anti-Hindutva forces are making the equation: civic nati onalism=secularism=good=nonviolent and tolerant of democracy, while in contrast, Hindutva forces are altering this equation to read: cultural nationalism=Hindu nationalism=good=nonviolent and tolerant of democracy.' She does challenge the assertions of both the groups as both these types have resorted to violence in different forms. She very well brings out the weaknesses of those who profess by secularism and in turn give a handle to its opponents, and in the process legitimise some of the acts of commission, which are indulged in by the communalists. While she is optimistic that the electoral system will force the communal parties to exercise restraint in their cultural policing, currently the latter at best can only be optimism. The case in point is Gujarat where they have 'successfully' done this cultural policing as an accompaniment of the anti Muslim pogrom.

Anwar Alam takes the theme further (*Secularism in India*-A Critique of Current Discourse). Alam is trying to answer the question as to why has the sixty years of 'practice' of secularism paved the way for communal fascism? He points out that the Indian state has relied on religion for its legitimacy and posits and that we cannot thwart the march of Hindu right just by defense of Nehuruvian secularism. One will like to state that Nehru cannot be blamed for all the ills of secular practice. The structure he inherited had a lot to do with this. To begin with, the Congress party itself was saddled with many a Hindutva elements. The soft Hidnutva individuals and opportunists were and are aplenty in the Congress. It was more a reflection of the incomplete secularisation process than any lack of understanding about secularism by Nehru, the individual. He himself was non-compromising but the whole machinery, which he headed, was infected by the communal virus, and could not overcome the structural obstacles for a correct practice of secular politics. Alam breaks the myths of Hinduism's 'tolerance', which is so much bandied about. He quotes Smith on this, 'beneath the logic of tradition of tolerance of Hinduism (read Brahminical Hinduism) lies the reality of a violent, exploitative and hierarchical caste system whose operation and practice have, historically led a vast section of humanity—not only scheduled castes but also a section of the poorest amongst the other backward castes—to live a dehumanised life and whose political assertion in recent times, thanks to democracy, is becoming intolerable for the upholders (mainly upper castes) of Brahminical Hinduism (p.92).' Very aptly Alam continues, 'It successfully countered the challenge of Buddhsims, Jainism and Sikhism by appropriating their symbols and reducing them to 'sects' of Hinduism. Similarly it successfully accommodates the revolt of the Bhakti movement in medieval period and the rise of Dalit movement in modern times within the dominant Brahminical fold(p.92).' Alam correctly shows the linkage between state and religion. The reviewer feels the use of the term 'Nehruvian secularism' for the practices of the Indian state is invalid. We must see the context. Also post-Nehru, there has been a degeneration of the practices as the successive Prime Ministers themselves resorted to the use of communal cards for their short-term gains, a phenomenon unthinkable in Nehru's time. No doubt even before the ascendance of the Sangh Parivar, the state did promote Brahminical ethos in the name of Hindu religion.

Alam does go into the details of the secularisation process and role of state in the same essay. One point, which is not generally given great attention, is the place of religion after the secularisation. Here mostly the word 'religion' is used as such, while what should be used is the role of the clergy. In a secular state, while the power of the clergy takes a back seat, the other aspects of religion are not dictated by the state. It becomes a personal matter, ie the clergy ceases to be the 'Guide' of state policies. The distinction is important as many a times there is a temptation to restrict religious practices (eg in post-revolutionary Soviet Russia). The personal practice of one's faith is perfectly valid in a secular state, while the borderline dividing the personal, social and political may be a bit blurred at times. These are the fuzzy zones where social debate, and not a divine ordinance, can come to resolve the tangle. Alam correctly laments the absence of serious attention to the deeper link between democracy and secularism and approvingly quotes Partha Chatterjee, ' ... or should the response (to the attacks on secularism) be a defense of the duty of a democratic state to ensure policies of religious tolerance? (p. 112)'

The attacks on missionaries, nuns, and priests scattered and working in far-flung areas, has been the major response of the Sangh Parivar to the assertion of Adivasis. Knowing well that educational activities of Missionaries empower the Adivasi; who in turn become more assertive in demanding their rights, and in threatening the status quo, disturbing the social support base of Sangh Parivar. That is the reason why the Parivar has unleashed a process of attacks on alleged 'forcible conversions'. Ghanshyam Shah, a keen observer of social processes of Gujarat, has contributed a longish essay on this theme. This essay does full justice to the problem under consideration and demonstrates the social dynamics of Gujarat to make his point.

Shah takes a detailed look at the social dynamics of Dangs, the district where maximum such anti-Chritstian violence took place. The role of communalised state apparatus, the rise in social presence of VHP and the patronage of the central government (2002) ruled by the BJP-led coalition comes out very well. It is true that though percent of Adivasis declared themselves as Hindus in the 1991 census, they do continue to be Animists to a great extent and their marriage rituals etc are very different from caste Hindus. Also the attempts to bring them to institutionalised and dominant Brahminical ideological framework of Hinduism are nothing but 'conversions' to Hinduism for political purpose. The essayist points out, 'As a part of their welfare programmes, some of these Christian organisations also provide help in the form of loans for buying seeds or leveling lands... Catholics who believe in the liberation theology are engaged in social welfare programmes. Proselytisation is not their priority. (p.129)' The anti-Christian campaign is well planned at all the levels, including boycott of those refusing to go for bath in hot springs as symbol of accepting Hinduism, and they are prohibited from drawing water from the village wells. The propaganda that the missionaries are doing conversions by force is as concocted as the stories that they are disfiguring the holy dieties of Hindus. The paper is very well researched and draws heavily from the fieldwork and reports of social activists working in the area.

'Religious Mobilisation and Sadhus in Politics: The idealized versus realpolitic' by Virginia Van Dyke breaks new grounds in analysing a very peculiar phenomenon of Indian society, the Sadhu, the wandering people in holy garb with no particular aim and goal in life. Their identification with religion has been well exploited by the VHP for its project of Hindu Rashtra. As such, the word has been used in diverse circumstances. Essentially, sadhu means a religious renunciate, an individual outside this world. In past, groups of sadhus had played very negative roles during India's freedom struggle. They did stand for a type of communal frenzy that resulted in partition riots. Many a sadhu has been fielded by the BJP in the electoral arena, with a good deal of success, but here '...voters who support sadhus running for office are, for most part, also motivated by specific interests; that is, they vote for sadhus on caste and party lines, rather than because of religious aura of the candidate. (p.147)' Interestingly, the fairly well rooted concept in popular mind that sadhus are exclusively reclusive and the idea that Hinduism is a pacifist, tolerant religion are of fairly recent constructs. VHP uses the term Saints for these sadhus, which is a misnomer according to the reviewer. The word 'saint' should be reserved for the religious people from subaltern traditions like the Bhakti and Sufi cults, for people who build the bridges between communities and not sow the poison of hatred against other communities. The cleverness of the VHP in 'mobilsing the sadhus as symbols of militant Hinduism has, of necessity, included the dissemination of putative history in order to assign them a new role: that of 'patriots' defending Hindu India against invaders. (p 153)' Though currently most of the sadhus have been roped in by the VHP for its political project of Hindu Rashtra, there are some who are working for the other caste outfits as well.

The two nation theory has been a bane of the subcontinent. And we are suffering the pangs of its political fallouts. On both sides of the divide, it affects society and polity. The dilemma of the state of Pakistan and its intellectuals is brought out well by Mubarak Ali (Pakistan's Search for Identity). As Pakistan was formed on the very basis of Islam, its identity is deeply entrenched in the same. Any attempt to overcome this narrow identity creates a backlash, every time such a talk is in the air. The result is the tragic fate of minorities. Many a scholar has suggested rebuilding the identity of Pakistan on territorial grounds to overcome the past acts of omission, and vicious sectarian conflicts, which are plaguing that nation.

On the whole, this festschrift to Asghar Ali Engineer is a valuable addition to the currently available resources on the subject of communal politics in South Asia. Also, the contributors give the updated version of the problem. The spectrum of issues covered is very impressive. As pointed out earlier, what is centrally and painfully missing is the evaluation of the RSS and the Hindu communal onslaught in India. At no time in the past was the country so ravaged by the ill effects of communalism as during the last two decades. Any compilation on the theme cannot do justice to the subject unless the Sangh Parivar's threat to Indian democracy is elaborated. Also an article on Bohra reform would have made it more apt as a volume of essays for Asgar Ali Engineer.

The Partition, A Tragedy

(Book Reviewed: *Inventing Boundaries: Gender, Politics and the Partition of India* Edited by Mushirul Hasan, Oxford University Press, New Delhi, 2000, Price Rs. 595, P. viii+393)

Partition has been a major tragedy which even today is casting its shadow on the politics of the subcontinent and its reflection lies in the Kashmir problem, MQM movement in Pakistan, in the prevalence of communal politics in Pakistan and the rise of the same in India. Mushirul Hasan, an academic of high calibre, has been addressing this issue for more than a decade. The present volume, Inventing Boundaries (IB), has significant inclusion of more recent historiographical debates while evaluating old theories of the mechanism of the Partition process and goes on to suggest fresh areas of research and inquiry. It incorporates significant contributions by outstanding academics and leaders.

Different major political forces took diverse attitude to this issue. The Communist Party supported the demand of Pakistan on the ground of nationality and expounded that there are two National bourgeoisies, Muslim and the Hindu. This flawed understanding had deep influence of Lenin's thesis at the second Congress of Comintern, defining Muslim League as the Party of Muslim Bourgeoisie and Indian National Congress as the party of Hindu National Bourgeoisie. Wearing the blinding blinkers of mechanistic Marxism, not giving importance to the realities of the country, they concluded that both these bourgeoisie parties are stooge of British Imperialism and so they should make a compromise for the 'National Democratic Revolution' (Sajjad Zaheer, 2000, 113.) This understanding totally ignored the fact that the national bourgeoisie was too weak and Muslim League in particular expressed the aspirations of zamindars more than the bourgeoisie. KM Ashraf did realise this mistake and stated that the Communist Party was misled by slogan of Self-Determination and mistook Muslim communalism for something representing the organised expression of 'Rehri-Pak-Pathan nationlities for self-determination'. (Quoted in Sarkar, 1997, ch.13.) A very apt realisation! Khwaja Ahmad Abbas, another leftist columnist, was more scathing in his criticism of the mistake of the Communist Party.

The class base of the demand for Pakistan has been well explained by various writers and prominent feudal lords themselves. Hasan is on the dot when taking the cue from many of the contributors, he points out that, 'The clamour for a separate nation, though pressed vigorously in the post-war years with much popular backing and enthusiasm, was raised not so much by the Muslim divines, many of whom were waiting on the fringe of Indian politics to intervene on behalf of Islam, but by the vociferous professional groups in UP, Bihar, the princely State of Hydrabad and small but upcoming trading and banking communities in Gujrat, Bombay, and Calcutta.(Hasan, 2000, p35)' Hasan defends the concept of composite nationalism to the hilt in line with the values of the freedom struggle and its undisputed leader, Mahatama Gandhi.

At political mobilisational levels, one of the big failures of the INC was not to take up Nehru's brainchild of Mass Contact Programme with Muslim masses. The failure to implement this in due course made more and more unwilling Muslims fall into the trap of the demand for Pakistan, and in due course, agree with the passing of the Pakistan resolution amongst cries of Allah-o-Akbar.

Hasan has meticulously chosen his material for this volume. Ambedkar's thoughts on Pakistan remains one of the most scholarly treatment on the subject. Ambedkar, in his pragmatic style, raises questions pertaining to the role of Hindu-Muslim Unity in the advancement of the interests of India, the path this unity should take, that of appeasement or settlement etc. Interestingly, after initial support to the idea of Pakistan, Ambedkar, in the revised version of the book, opposes the demand for Pakistan on the ground that this may lead to the creation of a parallel Hindu Raj which will be most disastrous for the Shudras, the dalits of India, something very prophetic. India is currently trying to save its soul and body from the practitioners of the politics of Hindutva-Hindu Rashtra.

The two essays on Gender issues, one by Urvashi Butalia and the other by Ritu Menon and Kamala Bhasin, are not only most heartrending but also highlight the plight of women in the patriarchal society where the identity of communities are made over the bodies of women. Their fate in communal violence is most pathetic. In the partition process, not only were they victims of mass rapes and abductions but even in the post-partition rehabilitation process, they were abandoned by their own kith and kin on the ground of loss of honor. This compilation also has significant themes like Businessmen and the Partition, how an economist looks at the process of vivisection of the country, and the attitude of the Jamiyyat-i-Ulama-i-Hind. The Aligarh University has been at the hub of the political happening in more ways than one and Hasan's own contribution in this volume examines this in depth.

One of the significant points of the book is probably to include creative writing on partition and making it a significant source of one's impressions about the tragedy suffered by the subcontinent. Saadat Hasan Manto's *Toba Tek Sing* is an all-time classic on the theme, his Black Margins presents deeper insights into the process in a most imaginative way. Alok Bhalla's interview with Bhism Sahani, another major literary figure contributing on the issue, is very revealing and is a must for the understanding of the dynamics of the communities faced with tragedies of such mammoth proportions. Some of the contributions in this section are fairly 'specialist' in the treatment of themes dealt with (Alok Rai and Alok Bhalla), but they do make important general observations which enrich our understanding of the subject.

While noting the stir caused by the impact of creative writing, Hasan does supplement an optimistic streak in the discourse while quoting Ali Sardar Jafri's optimism of the future relationship between these countries,

> *Tum aao Gulshan-i-Lahore se chaman bardosh*
> *Hum ayen subah Banaras ki roshni lekar*
> *Himalaya ki hawaon ki tajagi lekar,*
> *Phir uske bad ye puchen ke kaun dushman hai*
> (You come covered with flowers of the Garden of Lahore, We bring to you the light and radiance of the morning of Benaras, the freshness of the winds of the Himalayas, and then ask who the enemy is.)

All in all, Mushirul Hasan has been coming back to the same theme again and again but with every new contribution one can see the rich addition to the earlier understanding and more source material, which adds to our grasp of the issue.

References

KM Ashraf, Quoted in Sumit Sarkar, *Writing History Socially*, Oxford, New Delhi 1997, Ch.13.

Mushirul Hasan, *Inventing Boundries,* Oxford, New Delhi, 2000, p.35.

Sajjad Jaheer, *Inventing Boundaries*, Oxford, New Delhi, 2000,p.113.

Appendix

Comments

Professor Irfan Habib, a noted historian, has commented:

> One must remember that the priority before them was Independence. The partition was a secondary concern. They probably felt that once the British were out of the way, differences could be resolved, that Pakistan would not be a sustainable entity. There was a bit of misreading of the British imperialist agenda. Also, people forget that, over the years, the wars and wrangling over Kashmir has re-imposed the divide rather than dissolve it.

Riposte by **Narendra Singh Sarila,** Indian Diplomat & former ADC to Mountbatten and author of the book *The Shadow of the Great Game: The Untold Story of India's Partition*, writing in *The Tribune* of 19 August 2009, says:

> I am disappointed with Jaswant Singh's 660-page book on Jinnah and Partition, released earlier this week. At the end he (Jaswant Singh) says, 'I still fail to understand why India was partitioned in 1947? Or the manner in which it was done.'
>
> If, even after his massive research and hard work, Jaswant Singh did not get to the bottom of his subject, there is a reason for it. It is because he has ignored the most important element that was responsible for Partition, namely British strategic interests that required the creation of Pakistan. British top secret documents on Partition have now been declassified and there was no excuse for ignoring them. I myself showed these to him some years back. The whole story is there in those documents.
>
> The Labour government that came to power in Britain in mid-1945 was willing to grant independence to India but was worried about losing its 60-year-old military base here from which the British controlled the whole Indian Ocean area, including the eastern Middle-East that contained oil wells—The Wells of Power—of increasing importance in war and peace and which Stalin, with his rising ambition after his victory over Germany, the British feared, might seize. In the last two great wars it was from their Indian base that the British deployed Indian and British forces in Iran and Iraq and the British Chiefs of Staff were adamant on keeping a foothold in India. But Atlee, the British Prime Minister, knew that the government of a free India under the Congress party's rule would neither give them a military base nor join their team against the Soviet Union in the fresh Great Game. What were they to do?
>
> Towards the end of 1945, Field Marshal Wavell, the Viceroy of India, came up with a possible way out of their quandary. After the Congress party had refused to cooperate in the war effort in 1939, unless Britain announced that it would give freedom to India after the war, Wavell's predecessor, Lord Linlithgow, had encouraged Jinnah to formulate the

Pakistan scheme, informing London that Jinnah was in his pocket. 'He represents a minority and a minority can only hold its own with our assistance', the Viceroy told London.

Wavell now suggested that they use Jinnah's demand to create a separate state in the north-west—not give him all he wanted in the west but territories along Iran, Afghanistan and Sinkiang with the port of Karachi—and Pakistan would cooperate with them on defence matters. On being asked by London to give them a clear picture of the areas that could go to Pakistan, Wavell in a historic dispatch on February 6, 1946, sent a map delineating the boundaries of Pakistan he had in mind, which were exactly the boundaries that Radcliff drew 18 months later.

'So, what Pakistan was going to be was already decided in early 1946 and the time between then and August 15 was used by Atlee, Cripps and Wavell and later Mountbatten to make Jinnah accept the smaller Pakistan and the Congress party to accept Partition, while Atlee kept proclaiming from housetops that they were working to preserve India's unity.' All the British maneuvering can be discerned by studying the British top secret files. It is a myth that Jinnah founded Pakistan. President Roosevelt had posted his representative in Delhi after 1942 and his dispatches in the US archives also tell us much.

Some of the assessments in the book are also mistaken. To believe that the Cabinet Mission Plan would have resulted in a united India is moonshine. After 10 years Punjab, Sindh and the NWFP had the option to break away on one side and Bengal and Assam on the other side. That would give the League a much larger Pakistan after 10 years and certainly, in the meanwhile, it would fan the flames of communalism to prepare the ground for the above. And what about the princely states? They had the option to break away too. So, possibly Hyderabad would join Pakistan and would help reach Tripura and Manipur, which would be swallowed up. The Plan would have balkanized India and Nehru, despite the many mistakes he made, was correct in striking it down.

[As for an Indian federation, look at what has happened in Christian-Muslim Cyprus or divided Palestine.]

The Congress made many mistakes in the struggle, but Gandhiji united a heterogeneous and largely uneducated people, without which Independence was not possible.

I agree with Jaswant Singh that Jinnah at heart was a nationalist and a secularist. And he remained so for the first 60 years of his life—a long time. Jinnah opposed satyagrah, calling it an extreme programme that would lead to disaster. He was shunned by Gandhiji. And Motilal Nehru feared that this brilliant man would eclipse his son, Jawaharlal. In 1928 Jinnah proposed to convince the Muslims to give up separate electorates—that were preventing Hindu-Muslim political interdependence and unity—suggesting in return that Muslim representation in the Central Assembly be raised from 27 per cent to 33 per cent—a very minor concession compared to the possibility of ending the pernicious separate electorates. But he was pooh-poohed, and virtually driven out from the Congress party.

After the Congress refused to cooperate in the war effort in 1939, the Viceroy sought out Jinnah. The doctors had earlier the same year told him that he had terminal TB. Jinnah had always wanted to be the first in every thing. There are many instances in history of people abandoning their principles to achieve power and glory. So, for him it was now or never. His Pakistan scheme, launching Direct Action—the precursor of today's terrorism—and mobilising Muslims against the Hindus, were all in the pursuit of power and glory. He did not believe in what he was doing. After Pakistan had been achieved, he spoke in Karachi advocating secularism. But he quickly retreated when opposed by his followers.

Chagla, who worked with him in his law firm in Bombay, once told me that he was a man of great integrity. But it was tragic that at the end he lost it. And no man can be great without integrity. I also feel sympathy for Jinnah, for his humiliation and suffering. But at the end of his life he did many bad things, and inflicted incalculable harm. To believe that he was great just because he fought the mighty Congress party is nonsense. Do we call Hitler great because he fought the mighty Allies?

Comment by **Niloufer Bhagwat,** an eminent international jurist:

The restructuring and reorganisation of territories and boundaries of existing states/countries is one of the main instruments of Imperial control of resources and strategic territories; for this purpose some political and fascist organisations are set up and used. The killings which took place using so-called religious parties /cultural organizations on both sides, was both a preparation and a justification for the divide. In Iraq, as soon as the withdrawal of US troops is a part of the parliamentary agenda with the possibility of referendum being held, the killings once again are stepped up. When an Imperialist power is on the decline it is even more blood thirsty and ferocious. Today, it is not one power alone , it is the Banks, financial institutions and financiers at the core of the dominant system.

Jinnah, the Muslim League, the Jamait-e-Islami, the Tabligi Jammat were all collaborators political and cultural, whereas the Hindu extremist organisations played the same role as did some of the princely States. Gandhi's assassination was an Imperialist plot and the extremist organisations and their leaders who were a part of the wider plot received support from some of the Princely States.

There are familial and individual loyalties to the Ràj and to the Empire even to-day, which extends into several political parties of the right and left and into institutions and organisations overt and covert. Let us see how the narrative unfolds. The biggest threat to the unity and integrity of India continues to be from the same stream of finance capital operating from more than one capital.

It appears that Mumbai is once again to be targeted for attacks, the FBI was here inspecting railway stations and other regions duly escorted by policing agencies. The 'War of Terror' along with Swine flu is the new instruments of control even as the tatters of the economic policy of neoliberalism or the 'Washington Consensus' emerges globally.

In the context of India I was told by an intelligence operative that the decision making of the 'dirty tricks' department for the country has its headquarters in Mumbai. Now we can add New Delhi, Ahmedabad, Pune and Bangalore though earlier they were not as important.

It is a matter of immense satisfaction that those who make policy should directly witness its consequences and its impact on diverse sectors, institutions and on society as a whole.

The book and the controversies raised are diversionary, the Indian National Congress led by Mahatma Gandhi and Jawaharlal Nehru assisted by Sardar Vallabhai Patel, Maulana Azad, Khan Abdul Gaffar Khan, with the best will in the world could not have defeated partition, the decision was already taken, Pakistan would be the instrument of Anglo-American policy in the region and for better control it would have either proxies or military governments as an adjunct of the Empire.

Excerpts

(Review of) Jaswant Singh Book on Jinnah Revisits the 1947 Partition by K Gajendra Singh
http://www.boloji.com/analysis2/0478.htm
(Report of a panel discussion: Why are Indians Afraid of Faulting the Imperialist British.)

K Gajendra Singh was Indian ambassador to Turkey and Azerbaijan from August 1992 to April 1996. Prior to that, he served terms as ambassador to Jordan, Romania and Senegal. n a article (October 2006), The Mother Of All Battles: For Oil, Gajendra Singh writes in Information Clearing House, on *ME Oil and Partition of India:*

> An important reinforcement to Chomsky's conclusion (that US and Israeli interests coincide in the Middle East) has been clearly brought out in a well researched book by a retired Indian diplomat, Narendra Singh Sarila, *The Shadow of the Great Game: The Untold Story of India's Partition.* Sarila, who was briefly ADC to the last British Viceroy to India, Lord Mountbatten, in his book documents how the British leadership across the political spectrum, Conservatives and Labour, intrigued, told lies, divided the Indian subcontinent and created the state of Pakistan. Because Mahatma Gandhi, with his opposition to violence and war, and emphasis on peaceful means to resolve all disputes and Jawaharlal Nehru with his non-real political idealism and vision of creating friendship and understanding among colonised and exploited people of Asia, Africa, Middle East and elsewhere, would not join Western military pacts to protect from the Soviet Union, the oil resources in the Middle East dominated by Western powers.
>
> Sarila highlights, 'little known facts about the unobtrusive pressure that the USA exerted on Britain in favour of India's independence as well as unity in the hope of evolving a new post-colonial world order'. The British leaders warned Indian leaders against dollar domination. Sarila naively forgets what the US had done in Cuba and Philippines, after it replaced Spain as the colonial master.
>
> After the second world war, the British realised that they had to get out of India, but the subcontinent was a vital strategic asset, so till the end London tried to keep India as a dominion like Australia or Canada, to keep it as 'a base for Britain to continue their domination of the Indian Ocean and the oil-rich Persian Gulf with its wells of power', says the author. But as the 'Congress party of India would not play the great game with Britain against the Soviet Union', the British decided to partition India.
>
> The ultimate object was to retain at least some part in the north-west of India, 'for defensive and offensive action against the USSR in any future

dispensation in the sub-continent'. And Britain knew that this could be best achieved by having a willing and subservient Pakistan as its client. So the only way—was to use Jinnah to detach areas of India which border Iran, Afghanistan and Sinkiang and create a new state there. The author also traces the roots of the present Kashmir imbroglio and how the matter was dealt with in the UN to help out ally Pakistan.

Then there is another fine book by another retired Indian diplomat, C Dasgupta, *War and Diplomacy in Kashmir 1947-48.*

In war every truth has to have an escort of lies.

—Winston Churchil

K Gajendra Singh writing on *Hindustan's Geo-politic Strategic Mold: Only When United, India has Prospered,* says:

On the question of dominion status and independence for India in 1942, during the second world war, US President Franklin Roosevelt's envoy Averell Harriman was informed by the British that approximately 75 per cent of the Indian troops were Muslims but only 35 per cent of the troops were Muslims, Lord Wavell, the British Military Commander had cabled London the same week. Later, British Prime Minister Winston Churchill told Roosevelt in another context that, 'in war, every truth has to have an escort of lies', a hoary Western tradition over centuries. They excelled themselves in the US-led illegal invasion and occupation of Iraq. The escort of lies was so numerous that there was little truth left.

The divide and create mayhem policy used in the Indian subcontinent is being replicated in Iraq by Bush and Tony Blair, a wannabe Churchill, with the former claiming that Churchill was like a Texan. Sarila documents in detail how after the end of World War II in 1945, the new Labour government of Clement Attlee and Wavell decided to divide India. 'The British used Jinnah and political Islam to protect their strategic interests… This policy was the mother of all causes for the creation of Pakistan', asserts Sarila. They succeeded in selling the idea of a truncated Pakistan to Jinnah.

On June 3, 1947, British Foreign Secretary Ernest Bevin, while addressing the Labour Party's annual conference, spilled the beans that the division of India 'would help consolidate Britain in the Middle East'.

A British top secret appreciation prepared in the Commonwealth Relations Office, soon after Indian independence, now available in the India Office archives of the British Library, says: 'Financially, industrially and from the point of view of manpower and general material resources, India was stronger than Pakistan.' But that 'India had no real background on which to build and unite a nation, there being no real affinity between its North and South, the existence of disruptive elements like the Sikhs and the likelihood of the Communists, with their own agenda, growing in numbers and influence.'

On the other hand, the appreciation asserts that Pakistan, weak in financial and material resources—though comfortable in food and manpower—'has a definite background, Islam, on which to build up a nation and to unite the people...and has less to fear from internal disruptive forces than the government of India, and less to fear from secessionist tendencies.' [No thought of Bangladesh!]. So much for the so-called British political acumen!

Churchill and other British leaders had to be reminded by Indian leaders that their comments on such lines were unwarranted. Decades after 1947, the British media wrote obituary of elections and democracy in India, only to be proved wrong repeatedly.

The book sends out a cautionary signal to present-day Indians; to avoid misplaced idealism, superciliousness and escapism, to which some of their ancestors fell prey. New Delhi was a few years ago seduced by Washington (ask US allies Turkey and Pakistan , how they have been let down in the post-cold war period) into an nuclear agreement to enmesh India into the US spider's web which adversely affects the security of billion plus Indians. Throughout history, barring a few, the last one being Indira Gandhi, navel-watching Hindus have shown little strategic acumen.

With weak grassroots political organisations, Pakistan, with many British and the British-era civil servants, strengthened the bureaucracy's control over the polity. While the politicians wanted to strengthen relations with the British, Washington encouraged Military Chief General Ayub Khan to establish close cooperation with the Pentagon. And in 1958, the military took over power in Pakistan. USA, in pursuit of its national interests, has seldom bothered about the form of government in an ally. Otherwise, why did it embrace Pakistan, or say Egypt, Indonesia, Saudi Arabia or any of the other kingdoms and sheikhdoms and repressive regimes around the world? US talk of spreading liberty, freedom and democracy sounds hollow most times.

Beginning with Ayub Khan's unofficial visit to the US, the foundations for bilateral cooperation in the military field were laid. These have survived through thick and thin, like a bad marriage which neither side can let go, despite bad patches, like the initial takeovers by Generals Zia ul-Haq and Musharraf. But the 1979 entry of the Soviet troops into Afghanistan and 9/11 attacks on the US Trade Towers and Pentagon brought back the old romance. US finds military and other dictators easier to handle.

Conclusion

Many ignorant Indians, especially from the North, believe that the partition of the subcontinent in 1947 could have been avoided. Such colossal ignorance about history!

The White Christian Europe divided and destroyed the composite five-century old Ottoman empire using religion, ethnicity, language divide, even fooling the Arabs whose Caliph, the Ottoman Sultan, was resident in Istanbul. See how they have been divided, bullied, humiliated, destroyed and exploited since the First World War.

In the 1990s, non-Orthodox Christian US and NATO powers destroyed the multi-lingual, multi-ethnic and multi-religious South Slav Republic of Yugoslavia consisting of Serbs, Croats, Kosovars, Macedonians and others, who followed many religions. The Imperialists will do anything to gain control.

US-led illegal invasion of Iraq in 2003 and the brutal occupation has destroyed a united secular Iraq of Shia and Sunni Arabs and Kurds, Turkmen and others.

Seeing the level and kind of discussions in India, I feel dismayed that Indian media and think tanks remain brainwashed, even generationally, ie. those whose fathers studied in British schools and universities or British-style institutions in India, with their heroes in Clive, Hastings, Curzon, Churchill, Blair and now Bush and Obama.

Will Hindustan be ever free from the pernicious indoctrination by the white race, which still continues?

Bibliography

(from SACW.net)

The Big March: Migratory Flows After Partition of India
by Prashant Bharadwaj, Asim Kwaja and Atif Mian (*EPW*, August 30, 2008)

Book Review: *Partition Regrets*
Partition and the Making of the Mohajir Mindset: A Narrative by Brigadier AR Siddiqui (Oxord University Press Karachi, 172 pages)
by A G Noorani (*Frontline*, September 12, 2008)

Remembering Sylhet: A Forgotten Story of India's 1947 Partition
by Anindita Dasgupta (*EPW*, August 15, 2008)

Book Review: *Lines that divide peoples' hearts*
The Partition Motif in Contemporary Conflicts
Edited by Smita Tewari Jassal, Eyal Ben–Ari (Sage. Pages 381. Rs.480)
by Kanwalpreet (*Spectrum*, August 3, 2008)

Partition as conflict resolution
by Rita Manchanda (*Himal*, June 2008)

Metaphor, Memory, Myth: recasting partition as in Salil Choudhury, Manas Ray, Helene Cixous
by Tutun Mukherjee (*EPW*, May 10, 2008)

Book Review: *Can Partition be undone?*
Crisis in the Subcontinent: Partition, Can It Be Undone? by Lal Khan (Wellred Publications, London, 2001 / Lahore 2003 / Aakar Books, Delhi, 2007, pp225)
by Ranabir Sammadar (*EPW*, February 2, 2008)

The Long Partition and the Making of Modern South Asia: Refugees, Boundaries, Histories
by Vazira Fazila-Yacoobali Zamindar
(Columbia University Press, October, 2007, Cloth, 304 pages, 25 illus. ISBN: 978-0-231-13846-8)

Book Review: *The Human Cost*
The Great Partition: The Making of India and Pakistan by Yasmin Khan

(Viking, Penguin, Pages 251)
by AG Noorani (*Frontline*, October 6, 2007)

Book Review: *Path to Partition - a witness account*
An American Witness to India's Partition by Phillips Talbot (Sage, Pages 440)
by AG Noorani (*Frontline*, October 6, 2007)

The Psychiatrist's Partition
by Anirudh K Kala, Alok Sarin and Sanjeev Jain (in *Himal*, August 2007)

A Bloody March in 1947
by Ishtiaq Ahmed (*The News*, August 18, 2007)

Other Travails: Telling the story of the most neglected victims of Partition
by Ramachandra Guha (*The Telegraph*, August 18, 2007)

Would you like to visit Pakistan?
by Ravinder Kaur (*The Guardian* / Comment is Free, August 17, 2007)

Sixty years of Partition: Celebration or Lamentation
by K Z Islam (*The Daily Star*, August 17, 2007)

Freedom Came With A Price
by Ashis Nandy (*The Times of India*, August 16, 2007)

India and Pakistan: partition lessons
by Ravinder Kaur (*Open Democracy*, August 16, 2007)

A 60-year partition of minds
by Ayesha Siddiqa and Kuldip Nayar (*Rediff.com*, August 14, 2007)

60 years of remembering
by Pamela Philipose (T*he Indian Express*, August 13, 2007)

Expatriates question the 1947 partition
(in *The Times of India*, April 16, 2007]

Book Review: *Examining the great divide*
Partitions: Reshaping States and Minds
by Stefano Bianchini, Sanjay Chaturvedi, Rada Ivekovic and Ranabir.

Samaddar. Frank Cass, New York (First Indian reprint). Pages 176.
by VN Datta (*The Tribune*, April 1, 2007)

Book Review: *Memory, lived and forgotten*
Since 1947: *Partition Narratives among Punjabi Migrants of Delhi*
by Ravinder Kaur, Oxford University Press, 2007
by Urvashi Butalia (in *The Financial Express*, April 1, 2007)

Partition and the South Asian Diaspora: Extending the Subcontinent
by Papiya Ghosh
(Publisher: Routledge India, January 2007, 308pp. [ISBN-10: 0415424097])

Book Review: *Divided Memories*
Bengal Partition Stories: An Unclosed Chapter, edited by Dr Bashabi Fraser-Publisher Anthem, September 2006, ISBN (HB) 1843312255
by Santanu Sanyal (in *Business Line*, February 2, 2007)

A Tale of Two Cities: The Aftermath of Partition for Lahore and Amritsar 1947–1957
by Ian Talbot (*Modern Asian Studies,* Volume 41, Issue 01, January 2007, pp 151-185)

Book Review: *Surviving Liberation*
Torn from the Roots: A Partition Memoir, Kamla Patel, translated by Uma Randeria, Women Unlimited, 2006
by Jyoti Nair Belliappa (in Literary Review / *The Hindu*, December 3, 2006)

Partitions, memories and reconciliation
by Satya P Gautam (*Seminar,* November 2006)

Punjab, partition and Pakistan
by Iftikhar H Malik (*Seminar*, November 2006)

Book Review: *Letting Silence Speak*
Unsettling Partition: Literature, Gender and Memory by Jill Didur
by Karen Herland (in *Concordia Journal,* November 9, 2006)
Rehearsing the Partition: gendered violence in 'Aur Kitne Tukde'
by Jisha Menon *(Feminist Review,* Volume 84, Number 1, 2006, pp. 29-47-19)

Religious Differences had nothing to do with Partition
by Salil Mishra (*Kashmir Times*, September 16, 2006)

Pakistan scholar attempts to trace origin of Lohani Pathans
by Varinder Walia (*The Tribune*, August 24, 2006)

Birth Pangs
by Ashis Nandy (*The Times of India*, August 13, 2006)

The Last Journey:
Exploring Social Class in the 1947 Partition Migration
by Ravinder Kaur *(EPW,* June 3, 2006)

The Historiographical Operation:
Memory and History
by Ranabir Samaddar *(EPW*, June 3, 2006)

Gendering Oral History of Partition
by Anjali Bhardwaj Datta (*EPW*, June 3, 2006)

Book Review: *Partitions* by Kamleshwar, Penguin, Rs 350
Reviewed by Shams Afif Siddiqi (*The Telegraph*, May 26, 2006)

Book Review: *Coming to terms with history*
Partition Dialogues: Memories of a Lost Home
by Alok Bhalla, OUP, hardback, p.244, Rs. 395
by Keki N Daruwala (in: Literary Review *The Hindu,* May 07, 2006)

A Train to Karachi -II
by Amar Jaleel (in: Magazine Section *Dawn*, March 12, 2006)

Routine Violence: Nations, Fragments, Histories
by Gyanendra Pandey (Published in 2006 by Stanford University Press/ Permanent Black)

Manto's Open It: Engendering Partition Narratives
by Sarvar V Sherry Chand (*EPW,* January 28, 2006)

Book Review: *Old Maps and New : Legacies of the Partition : A Pakistan Diary*
by Kavita Panjabi(Calcutta, Seagull Books, 2005 | ISBN : 8170462223)
by Debali Mookerjea-Leonard (*The Book Review*, December 2005)

Partition, Migration and Exile: Ritwik Ghatak and the Constitution of the Cinematic Signifier
by Anuradha Ghosh (a paper presented in the UGC – National Seminar on Diasporic Studies: Theory, Literature and Arts, December 15-16, 2005, held at Guru Nanak Dev University, Amritsar.)

Book Review: *Ongoing History. Continuing Effects*
by Ramya Sreenivasan (*H-Gender-MidEast,* January, 2005) Ritu Menon, ed. *No Woman's Land: Women from Pakistan, India and Bangladesh Write on the Partition of India.* New Delhi: Women Unlimited, 2004.

Could Partition have been made less bloody?
by Ramachandra Guha

(Magazine Section-*The Hindu,* August 28, 2005)
Partition and Many Nationalisms
by Nonica Datta [*EPW,* July 15, 2005]

Book Review: *Community Problems*
Life After Partition: Migration, Community and Strife in Sindh, 1947-1962
by Sarah Ansari (Oxford University Press, Karachi, Pages: 240, Price: Rs 395)
by Tariq Rahman (June 19, 2005)

Book Review: *Heroines from a Lost Homeland*
Coming Out of Partition: Refugee Women of Bengal by Gargi Chakravarty - Bluejay Books, New Delhi, 2005, pp 200
by Sumanta Banerjee (*EPW,* April 23, 2005)

Woman and homeland in Ritwik Ghatak's films: Constructing post-Independence Bengali cultural identity
by Erin O'Donnell *(Jump Cut,* Winter 2005)

Introduction: Mourning and Memory
by Rebecca Saunders and Kamran Aghaie (Comparative Studies of South Asia Africa and the Middle East, 2005; 25: 17-29)

Gender, Memory, Trauma: Women's Novels on the Partition of India
by Ananya Jahanara Kabir (*Comparative Studies of South Asia, Africa and the Middle East* - Volume 25, Number 1, 2005, pp. 177-190)

Generations of Memory: Remembering Partition in India/Pakistan and Israel/Palestine
by Jonathan D Greenberg (*Comparative Studies of South Asia, Africa and the Middle East*, 2005; 25: 89-110)

Quarantined: Women and the Partition
by Debali Mookerjea-Leonard (*Comparative Studies of South Asia Africa and the Middle East*, 2004; 24: 35-50)

Nostalgia of 'Desh', Memories of Partition
by Anasua Basu Raychaudhury (*EPW*, December 25, 2004)

Violence, Displacement and the Issue of Identity-1947
(Concurrent Session A-2 | SDPI Conference Islamabad, December 2004)

Book Review: *The Trauma and the Triumph: Gender and Partition in Eastern India* edited by Jasodhara Bagchi and Subhoranjan Dasgupta; published by Stree, Kolkata 2003; pp 272, Rs 500
by Tanika Sarkar (*Seminar*, December 2004)

Book Review: *Partition and Its Meanings*
The Trauma and the Triumph: Gender and Partition in Eastern India
edited by Jasodhara Bagchi and Subhoranjan Dasgupta;
published by Stree, Kolkata 2003; pp 272, Rs 500.
by Himani Bannerji (*EPW*, August 21, 2004)

Book Review: *The Aftermath of Partition in South Asia*
by Tai Yong Tan and Gyanesh Kudaisya.
Reviewed by Sarah Ansari (*Pacific Affairs*, Summer 2004, Vol 77, No 2)

Forced Migration and Ethnic Cleansing in Lahore in 1947: Some First Person Accounts
by Ishtiaq Ahmed (June 2004)

Cinema's taboo on partition
by Mehboob Khan (BBC, 11 June, 2004)

*Divided families and the making of nationhood in India and Pakistan, 1947--1965*by Vazira Zamindar, PhD Dissertation, Columbia University, 2003. *Download the dissertation* (PDF Format)-(Only accesible to Columbia affiliates).

The arrival impact of Partition refugees in Uttar Pradesh, 1947-52
by Yasmin Khan (*Contemporary South Asia*, 12:4, 2003)

Legacy of a Divided Nation: A Book reveiw of Witness to Partition: A Memoir by BR Nanda
by Arnab Bhattacharya (*The Telegraph,* November 21, 2003)

'I am Not a Refugee': Rethinking Partition Migration
by Md. Mahbubar Rahman and Willem Van Schendel (*Modern Asian Studies*, 37, 3, 2003, pp.551-584.)

Borders and Boundaries in Partition Literature
by Shivam Vij (September 2003)

Book Review: *Pointers to Partition*
A Narrative of Communal Politics: Uttar Pradesh, 1937-39 by Salil Misra; Sage, New Delhi, 2001; pp 363, Rs 295.
by Gyanesh Kudaisya (June 2003)

Midnight's Children Humanities Festival-Teach-In on *Thirty Years of Indian and Pakistani History: A Tryst with Destiny* (March 6 , 2003)
Speaker: Aamir Mufti
Speaker: Gyan Pandey

Partition: Why shy away from debate?
by Dr Iftikhar H Malik (August 20, 2002)

Social Roots of Partition Process
by Ram Puniyani (*SACW,* February 17, 2002)

Partition Revisited - A Letter to the Editor
by Rajindar Sachar (*Times of India*, January 27, 2003)

The Partition debate - I
by Mushirul Hasan (*The Hindu,* January 02, 2002)

The Partition debate - II
by Mushirul Hasan (*The Hindu,* January 03, 2002)

Memories of a Fragmented Nation: Rewriting the Histories of India's Partition by Mushirul Hasan [ND]

Moment of Parting
by Dipankar Gupta (*The Telegraph,* February 4, 2002)

The 1947 Partition of India:
A Paradigm for Pathological Politics in India and Pakistan
by Ishtiaq Ahmed

Cripps and India's Partition
by AG Noorani (*Frontline*, 20 - August 02, 2002)

Cripps and India's Partition-II
by AG Noorani (*Frontline,* August 3 - 16, 2002)

Misreading Partition Road Signs
by Hamza Alavi (November 2002)

India and Pakistan,1947-2002
by Gyanendra Pandey (March 2002)

[The Introductory Essay] *Remembering Partition: Violence, Nationalism an History in India*
by Gyanendra Pandey

Book Review: *Retelling History*
Pangs of Partition, Volume I: The Parting of Ways, and Volume II: The Human Dimension edited by S Settar and Indira Baptista Gupta; Indian Council of Historical Research, Manohar, New Delhi, 2002; pp 368+358, Rs 700 each.
by Charu Gupta (April 2002)

Porus Border, Divided Selves: A symposium on Partitions in the East
(A special issue of *Seminar*, February 2002)

The 1947 Partition: Drawing the Indo-Pakistani Boundary
by Lucy Chester (January 2002)

Review Article: The Partition of India
by AG Noorani (December 22, 2001)

Les partitions comparées
by R Ivekovic (Actes du VIII ème
Congrès de l'Association pour la Recherche InterCulturelle (ARIC)

Univ ersité de Genève - 24-28 septembre 2001)

India and Partition
by Nandini Gooptu [2001]

Jinnah: Making a myth
by Mubarak Ali

Changing Borders, Shifting Loyalties:
Religion, Caste and the Partition of Bengal in 1947
by Sekhar Bandyopadhyay

Memory, History and Fictional Representations of the Partition
by Alok Bhalla

Partition Memories, 'Minorization' and discourses of rootedness in Jharkhand: A comparison of cross border displaced and 'invisible refugees' in Ranchi district
by Kathinka Sinha-Kerkhoff

Interrogating Victimhood: East Bengali Refugee Narratives of Communal Violence
by Nilanjana Chatterjee [PDF]

Sagas of Victory / Memories of Defeat?: The Long Afterlife of an Indo-Muslim Warrior Saint, c. 1033 - 2000
by Shahid Amin [A Real Video File]

The Persistence of Memory:
The Search for Truth, Justice, and Reconciliation
by Urvashi Butalia [A Real Video File]

A Finer Balance
by Dilip Simeon [A Real Video File]

Bengali State, Nation and Religious Identity: Conflicting Identifications and Multiple Meanings
by Shelly Feldman

Partition of the Indian Subcontinent, Special issue Interventions: *International Journal of Post-colonial Studies*, Vol 1, No 2, 1999
edited by Ritu Menon

The Fashioning of a Frontier: The Radcliffe Line and Bengal's Border Landscape, 1947-52
by Joya Chatterji *(Modern Asian Studies*, January 1999)

Nation, Reason and Religion: The Punjab's Role in the Partition of India
by Ayesha Jalal *(EPW,* August 8,1998)

Partition of India and Punjabi Novel
by Chaman Lal (in *Partition of India: Literary Responses*, Edited by SR Chakravarty, Mazhar Hussain. New Delhi: Har-Anand, 1998)

Fragments of Imagination: Rethinking the Literary in Historiography through Narratives of India's Partition
by Jill Didur (*Jouvert*, Vol.1, No.2 1997)

The Troubled History of Partition
by Radha Kumar
(Foreign Affairs, January/ February 1997)

Secularists, Subalterns and the Stigma of 'Communalism': Partition Historiography Revisited
by Ayesha Jalal (Modern Asian Studies, 30, 3 1996, pp.681-737)

Remembered Villages: Representation of Hindu-Bengali Memories in the Aftermath of Partition
by Dipesh Chakrabarty (*Economic and Political Weekly*, August 10, 1996)

Subcontinental Divide:
A study of the effects of Partition on India's people.
by Akash Kapur

History, Nation and Community: Reflections on Nationalist Historiography of India and Pakistan
by Rajeev Bhargava

Azad Jinnah and Partition [A review article]
by Ayesha Jalal (May 1989)

The Legacy Project: Legacy Events Index
India - Pakistan Partition

The past in the present: India, Pakistan and history
by Maruf Khwaja

Freedom in an idiom of loss
by Jasodhara Bagchi (2002)

The Partitions of Memory
The Afterlife of the Division of India
Edited by Suvir Kaul
See Review article: *New perspectives on Partition* by Naunidhi Kaur

Pakistan or Partition of India
by B R Ambedkar (1945)

Films

The Cloud-Capped Star (Meghey Dhaka Tara)
Directed by Ritwik Ghatak.
1960, 35mm, b/w, 126 min
Garam Hawa
by Directed by MS Sathyu, 1973 (An important film on the Partition of India -1947) [short excerpt on Youtube]
The Division of Hearts (A documentary on Partition by Peter Chappel and Sati Khanna)
Mammo (A valuable film on Partition by Shyam Benegal, 1994/130 mins)
Khamosh Pani (A film by Subiha Sumar)
Earth (A film by Deepa Mehta)
Tamas (A Television series based on the writing of Bhisham Sahni)
Partition (A film by Tariq Ali and McMullen)
Earth (based on Pakistani novelist Bapsi Sidwa's Cracking India on the political dynamics of the India/Pakistan 1947 partition)
Karvaan a film by Pankaj Butalia (1999)
A Review of the film Karvaan
Train to Pakistan
Stories of the Broken Self (a documentary by Furrukh Khan)
*Rabba Hun Kee Kariye (*Thus Departed our Neighbours) (65')
a film by Ajay Bhardwaj on 1947 recounted in *Countryside Punjab*
Partition Footage from CNN
1.9M/44 sec. QuickTime moviw
4M/44 sec. QuickTime movie
Partition-The Day India Burned (A BBC documentary)
The Sky Below (75')
2006/07, directed by Sara Singh
(The India-Pakistan frontier six decades after Partition)
Rabba Hun Kee Kariye (65')
2007, directed by Ajay Bhardwaj
(The scars of Partition in Indian Punjab)